To Francesca,
Live the code!

2022

THE CODE

"Shaun Tomson has written an important and engaging book filled with wisdom and practical advice about personal growth and overcoming the inevitable challenges adolescents and young adults everywhere face. All adolescents, all parents, and better still all adolescents and their parents together would do well to read and ponder the inspiration and lessons contained in these pages."

—*Michael Weitzman, MD, Professor of Pediatrics and Psychiatry, New York University School of Medicine*

"Shaun has simplified some very important concepts that are relevant to each and every one of our kids. He relates these concepts in stories to his work as a surfing professional, encouraging our youth to where they are motivated to act in a positive manner. 'I will' is a resounding mantra for youth of today. This is a great piece of literature that I humbly suggest is read by our children and their parents. Together they can and will change the world."

—*David Edelman, MA, MBA, MFCC, President, Board of Directors, Santa Barbara Boys and Girls Club*

"Shaun's candidly unique insights into his ride provide hope and promise to new generations in following their dreams on their own personal wave."

—*Diana Starr Langley, Chair, Board of Directors, United Boys and Girls Clubs of Santa Barbara County*

"Often, the story of a champion in sport is characterized by determination, focus, commitment and dedication and that is indeed true with Shaun. However, Shaun's insights are much more powerful and inspiring because they transcend competition and apply to all of our lives. Through the power of 'I will' comes the call to live a connected, purposeful and principled life."

—*Jim Weber, CEO, Brooks Running*

"*The Code* is a guide for self-empowering decision making and provides the tools to effect positive change. It draws on Shaun's life experiences as both a world champion surfer and a father, giving insight and inspiration to young minds."

—*Pat O'Neill, President and CEO, O'Neill Wetsuits*

"The world today is very much like a wave: it's shifting and changing virtually every second. Like surfers, we are defined by the decisions we make in this dynamic environment. Shaun draws on a life of learning, both on waves and off, and offers some sage advice for drawing the best line through life. I love this book."

—*Jim Moriarty, CEO, Surfrider Foundation*

"Shaun Tomson will always be a surfing legend, but if history is just he'll be equally revered for his work out of the water. *The Code* cements his status as one of surfing's great thinkers and its lessons carry weight and value for everyone."

—*Brendon Thomas, Editor,* Surfer Magazine

THE CODE
THE POWER OF "I WILL"

BY
WORLD-CHAMPION SURFER
SHAUN TOMSON
WITH PATRICK MOSER

GIBBS SMITH
TO ENRICH AND INSPIRE HUMANKIND

First Edition
22 21   9 8

Published by
Gibbs Smith
P.O. Box 667
Layton, Utah 84041

1.800.835.4993 orders
www.gibbs-smith.com

Designed by Andrew Brozyna
Printed and bound in China
Gibbs Smith books are printed on either recycled, 100% post-consumer waste, FSC-certified papers or on paper produced from sustainable PEFC-certified forest/controlled wood source. Learn more at www.pefc.org.

Library of Congress Cataloging-in-Publication Data

Tomson, Shaun.
 The code : the power of "I will" / Shaun Tomson with Patrick Moser. — First edition.
    pages cm
  ISBN 978-1-4236-3429-4
1. Tomson, Shaun. 2. Surfers—South Africa—Biography. 3. Self-realization. I. Moser, Patrick (Patrick J.), 1963- II. Title.
  GV838.T66A3 2013
  797.3'2092—dc23
  [B]
                    2013005922

CONTENTS

INTRODUCTION

A number of years ago a surfing friend of mine, Glenn Hening, invited a group of kids to a surf contest at my adopted home beach of Rincon, a famous break that straddles the county lines of Santa Barbara and Ventura in Southern California. Glenn is also a teacher and environmentalist, and Rincon was facing a severe sewage problem during winter rains—the time of year Rincon breaks best. He was holding an event to bring attention to the issue and to encourage homeowners along the beach to modernize their aging septic systems and help clean up the water. He asked me to present each kid with a keepsake to remember the day—something that would encourage them to become more environmentally aware—and he gave me a budget of $120.

My wife, Carla, and I ran an apparel company at the time— Solitude—and it would have been easy for me to grab some gear for the kids or use my contacts in the surf industry to get a pile of surf-related products donated. Instead I went home, sat down in front of my laptop, and quickly wrote out the twelve most important lessons that surfing had taught me about life: twelve lines, 105 words, each lesson beginning with the words "I Will." It was all done in twenty minutes. I had no fixed objective, no targeted number of words, just the idea of getting something down that I thought would be useful and important to these young people. The lessons fell into a natural order, one by one, like a twelve-wave set that I've often seen at my favorite break in the world, Jeffreys Bay in South Africa. When I was finished I titled the lessons "Surfer's Code."

I had the lessons printed onto one hundred plastic cards at a local shop, and it cost me $120—right on budget. I handed them out to the kids at the event. I told them that I didn't create the code, I simply wrote down lessons that were already out there—in my heart and in the hearts of many surfers—but that sometimes get overlooked in our busy lives. After my little talk the kids asked me for more cards for their friends and family.

The cards turned into a groundswell, and I began giving talks at various schools and other gatherings about the life lessons that surfing had taught me. I handed out more cards and even put them in the pockets of the boardshorts that were in our Solitude clothing line. The talks eventually evolved into a book called *Surfer's Code*, in which I told the stories I'd learned from traveling around the oceans of the world and how I used surfing as a metaphor for riding the waves of life. I gave motivational talks from Las Vegas and Abu Dhabi to Johannesburg. I spoke to multinational corporations like Disney, Cisco, and General Motors, and I shared the stage with successful businessman Sir Richard Branson and best-selling author Malcolm Gladwell. No matter the audience I always stressed the fundamental lessons that surfing had taught me about life. I talked about a simple code I had learned that helped me deal with fear, defeat, and personal tragedy.

This book was inspired not by the surf or by my international speaking engagements but by a small group of kids I spoke with at Anacapa School in Santa Barbara, California. I'd been invited to give a talk by Headmaster Gordon Sichi, a surfer I met out at Rincon one day. After I spoke with the students and engaged in some lively discussion, I decided to give them an assignment. I told them I'd written the original Surfer's Code in twenty minutes—a quick exercise to capture the essence of what was important to me. I told them, "Create your own code. Take twenty minutes and tell me about all your goals. Begin every sentence with the words 'I Will.'" About a week later Gordon sent me their answers. They were beautiful, sensitive, full of humor and hope. In essence the kids wrote a series of promises they had made to themselves.

This book is about many things—faith, courage, creativity, determination—but above all it's about the promises we make to ourselves about the future. I hope these stories will inspire you to believe in yourself and to believe in the power that each and every one of us has to effect change through the power of "I Will." Once you do that, you begin to shape your future and achieve whatever you wish for.

—Shaun Tomson

Photograph by Lance Trout.

1.

I WILL BE MYSELF

Chasing the dragon sounds exciting. It conjures up adventure in far-off places and the chance to experience something new. I didn't know about the drug references. I didn't know the chase could involve addiction and sudden death.

My new friend—I'll call him John—sat on the edge of his bed moving a lighter under some aluminum foil. When it started to smoke he leaned over with a straw and inhaled the fumes.

"Hey, Shaun," he said. "You gotta try this. All the guys at Pipeline are doing it."

"What is it?" I'd just come up to his room from downstairs.

"China white."

I'd never seen someone use heroin up close. There were guys back home in South Africa who took drugs on the beach in Durban where I grew up, but my father kept us away from them. A well-known surfer of the time—the first South African to win a contest in Hawai'i—ended up getting arrested for smuggling drugs, so he became an example for us of what not to do. Overall I had a pretty sheltered upbringing. I knew about drugs, but I'd never tried them. I was nineteen years old when John asked me to chase the dragon—to sit down next to him and try what all his friends were trying. I was in Hawai'i, on the North Shore of O'ahu, 12,000 miles from my parents and my home. I'd just finished my first year at the University of Natal and would be surfing for the next three months with John and his friends. We were all about the same age, and I wanted to make a good impression on them. I wanted to fit in.

⁞⋁⋀⋁⋀⋁⋀⋁⋀⋁⋀⋀

I'd been to Hawai'i before—the first time back in 1969, a bar mitzvah present from my dad—but this was my first chance to spend the whole winter season there. It was November 1974, and if you wanted to make your mark in the surf world at that time, you had to come to the North Shore and take on the biggest waves at places like Waimea Bay, Sunset Beach, and Pipeline. That's where John and his friends surfed. I'd just met John—I'd rented a little room off his parents' main house in Pupukea—but I wanted to know him better because he was a good surfer at a break where I wanted to be a good surfer.

You have to understand: you don't just drive up to these beaches, paddle out, and surf the waves. You have to get to know the people who live and surf there. They have local knowledge, stuff you can't read about in books or magazines—when to paddle out, where to sit in the lineup, how to avoid riptides that will suck you out to sea or the shallow parts of the coral reef that will give you a potentially fatal head wound. People still die surfing Pipeline today. It's one of the world's most dangerous waves, and the best way not to get hurt is to talk to the locals and show them you respect all the knowledge that's taken them years to learn the hard way. So obviously that's what I wanted to do with John. He'd grown up there and had all the inside knowledge.

But I wanted even more: not just to survive those waves, but to charge them. To be the best. There was no real money in surfing back in 1974. We had individual contests around the world—in Australia, California, Hawai'i, and my home in South Africa—but you couldn't make a living at it. Not like today. Professional surfers can now make millions of dollars through contests on the World Tour and sponsorship with companies like Nike, Quiksilver, Billabong, and O'Neill. They're finally making the kind of money they deserve, because they put their lives on the line in those waves. Forty years ago that wasn't the case. Those of us who entered contests paddled out for two things: notoriety and prestige. We wanted to be the best and get our pictures in the magazines, and that meant going to Hawai'i for three months and showing the whole surf world that we belonged. If you want to take the ultimate climb, you go to Mount Everest. If you want to be the best in sports, you go to the Olympics. Our Mount Everest, our Olympics, was Hawai'i.

I was a nobody when I arrived. Or almost nobody. I'd finished my first year of college in Durban—our school year runs February to November—taking classes in accounting, business administration, mathematics, and Roman Dutch law. I wasn't really sure what field I wanted to get into, but I'd made a good start in my classes. I also grew up surfing. My father had always encouraged me in that area, and I'd won a pro contest that gave me enough money to travel to Hawai'i as soon as classes were done and rent a cheap room from John's parents. I bought a rusted-out car for $150 when I got there so I could travel the seven miles between Haleiwa and Sunset Beach. These were the proving grounds on the North Shore, the home of all the famous breaks I'd read about in the magazines and watched in the surf movies.

Ian Cairns, a well-known Australian surfer—he'd won contests in Hawai'i and made the cover of *Surfer* magazine, which was a huge deal at the time—told me after my contest win in South Africa: "Shaun, you should come to Hawai'i for the winter." When someone you look up to and respect encourages you, it's easy to be influenced by them. In Ian's case it's what I'd call positive peer pressure: we shared the same values and were working hard toward the same goal—to be the hottest surfer in the world. Ian knew there was only one place to go to make that happen, and he encouraged me.

SOMETIMES SMALL DECISIONS— CHOICES YOU MAKE IN AN INSTANT—HAVE SUCH HEAVY CONSEQUENCES.

There's also negative peer pressure, of course, and that can be just as powerful. But it's easy to miss the danger hidden in negative peer pressure. Sometimes you don't even see it coming. A few nice words from someone you've just met, a friendly person interested in the same things you are, who likes the same music, who likes to go new places. And it's not that they mean you any harm. Their friends are doing it, and maybe they want to be cool. Or maybe they're just curious and out to try something new. They're not looking to get you into trouble, but they're not necessarily looking out for your best interests either. Life gets boring sometimes, we all know it. You want to shake things up. You want to have an adventure.

John was being friendly that day. He was a good guy and a gifted surfer. I was a new face in the neighborhood, and he probably wanted me to feel welcome in his home and on the North Shore. His room was a normal teenager's room. I'd walked up the stairs and noticed he had some pot plants growing outside on a patio, which caught my attention. But there was nothing evil about the place, nothing dark or scary. "Here's something I'm digging," John would've said in the slang of the day. "Maybe you'll dig it too." And he offered me the heroin.

That was it. There was no group of people yelling at me, forcing me to do something I didn't want to do, pushing me to act like them or to prove myself. This was just John and me in his room, a couple of teenagers hanging out together. It was an everyday moment, and what I did at that moment changed the rest of my life. Sometimes small decisions—choices you make in an instant—have such heavy consequences. I recognize that now. At the time it didn't seem like such a big deal. I knew why I was in Hawai'i. I knew what I wanted to achieve, and doing heroin wasn't any part of that. I watched John inhaling fumes, and I turned away.

It was easy to say no. I wanted John to like me. I wanted to be cool and fit in with him and his group of friends. My saying no didn't bother him any, and we didn't talk about it after that day. We surfed together a few times. A week or so later I found a new place to live, and I didn't really see John around the rest of the winter, which was a little odd. But I was moving in a different direction. It was an amazing period of personal growth for me. I learned how to charge the most difficult waves in the

The North Shore of O'ahu, Hawai'i, November, 1974—
twelve months out of the South African Army and a
few weeks after completing my first-year university
examinations. A teenager a long way from home.
Photograph by Dan Merkel.

world over the next three months. The experience also planted the initial seeds not only of the first professional surf tour that came into being two years later, but of my rise to world champion in 1977. I wouldn't have experienced either of those if I hadn't committed myself to spending the whole winter surfing on the North Shore.

After I got back to South Africa to start my second year at college, I heard John had died of an overdose. I felt terrible for him and his family—they'd taken me in when I'd first arrived and given me a place to stay. John had surfed so well the days we'd gone out together, and now he was gone.

So that's part of my story. As I say, at the time saying no didn't seem like such a big deal to me. Taking drugs wasn't a part of who I was, so it was easy to be myself and say no. But sometimes it can be really hard to say no in those circumstances. You have to think about who you are and what you stand for—what's right and what's wrong. These are the things parents and teachers and other people remind you of day in, day out. You probably agree with them most of the time and want to do the right thing.

What's hard sometimes is recognizing which decisions can change your life. Or end it. These decisions come up every day, everywhere: at school and at home; on the beach, or hanging out with your friends. They never stop. You want to have fun, you want to try something new, you want people to like you. Who doesn't? A lot of noise surrounds you in these situations, a kind of music that takes over, upbeat and exciting; it pumps you up and pulls you along, promises adventure. It's easy to get distracted and not listen to yourself.

My son Mathew died at home when he was fifteen, playing a dangerous game called the choking game. He was alone. He was a beautiful boy, and I'm sure he wanted to do the right thing and just didn't realize the danger he was in. Mathew is a big reason why I tell these stories. I tell them not just for him, and for myself and my wife, but because what happened to him holds meaning for others. I speak to a lot of young people these days, and I tell them to think twice before they act. It's something they've all heard before and sometimes they'll roll their eyes, but I tell them anyway because it's important. One day they'll be faced with a moment like I was in Hawai'i—or Mathew was at home—and that moment will change their lives. I tell them, "Take a moment to listen to yourself, to *be* yourself. Not what you think others may want you to be. Think about the repercussions. *Think twice.* If you do that, you'll make the right decision."

2.

I WILL DREAM

No professional world tour existed for surfers in 1975. We had contests here and there with a small amount of prize money, but no one made a living traveling the world as a surfer. And because no one did it, no one really thought it could be done.

Except a few dreamers.

We were young. It was late February on the North Shore of O'ahu—the end of the winter surf season—and Rabbit Bartholomew (an Australian) and I were standing at Ehukai Beach Park watching twelve-foot swells peaking over Pipeline's empty second reef. We'd both had fantastic seasons in the Hawaiian contests. In three months we'd gone from nobodies to being recognized as two of the hottest surfers in the world. I won the world championship two years later, in 1977; Rabbit won it the year after me. By that time the pro tour was in full swing, and our dream of turning a lifestyle into a living was coming true.

Discussing the future with my great rival and friend Wayne "Rabbit" Bartholomew on the beach at the Banzai Pipeline in Hawai'i, 1975. Photograph by Dan Merkel.

But on the beach that day at Ehukai the pro tour was pure imagination. We watched this last big swell of the season roll in and talked about whether to paddle out. We also talked about our futures. I was headed back to South Africa to take a law degree at the University of Natal in Durban. I asked Rabbit about his plans.

"I'm going to be a pro surfer, mate. I'm taking this dream and running with it."

Pro surfer. Sometimes you only need to hear someone say it out loud. Sometimes you only need to say it to yourself to make a dream come true.

Where do dreams begin? For Rabbit it began in hardship on the Gold Coast of Australia: parents' divorce, poverty, and eviction. The silver lining was that he ended up living by the beach and surfing a lot to stay out of trouble. By the time he was finishing Miami High School, he'd already decided he wanted to be the best surfer in the world. The only problem was, the last contest to decide a world champion took place in 1972 in San Diego, California. It was nearing the end of the Vietnam War at that time, and many young people—surfers included—had turned away from competition and organized sports. Rabbit's dream was like this beautiful painting with nowhere to hang it and no one around to admire it.

Of course, Rabbit wasn't going to let that stop him. The North Shore of Oʻahu was the center of the surf world in those days, especially Sunset Beach and Pipeline. All the best photographers hung out at those beaches, and getting your picture in the magazines—on the cover, best of all—was a way to make a name for yourself and get invited to the all-important Hawaiian contests. The surfers who won those contests also won the respect of their peers and were considered the best in the world. Here's how Rabbit tells the story of chasing his dream in his book *Bustin' Down the Door*:

> *I remember in early '73 I decided to do something about it, so I put on my best pair of board shorts, and my only clean shirt and I strode confidently into the Commonwealth Bank at Coolangatta ... to have my five minutes with the manager of the bank. And basically, I said, "Sir, I'm a professional surfer and I need $500 because I've got to be in Hawaii because that's where my future lies." Well he looked down the end of his glasses at me and said, "You've got*

*to be joking, mate," … and I walked out of the
bank and I didn't get a brass razoo. But at least
I knew exactly where I was beginning, and that
was nowhere.*

Rabbit scraped together enough money by working odd jobs and got his plane ticket to Hawaiʻi. He didn't know where he was going to stay, what he was going to eat, or how he was going to get along once he got there. What he did know was that the only way to get from nowhere to somewhere was to believe in yourself and take a chance.

For me, my dreams started in South Africa, not in poverty but in pride. From a very young age I approached surfing with the belief that it was a professional sport—my dad was a founder of the Gunston 500 in 1969 (then called the Durban 500), a contest I won for the first time in 1973. I've always been extremely proud to be a surfer, and I was proud to win that contest. Because my dad was involved in organizing the event, a local crew got really upset and believed that I'd won due to his influence. They yelled things like "biased judging" and "rigged event." As the crowd started to leave, the local crew hung up a big banner that read TOMSONS GO HOME. They also scrawled messages on the cement walls of the outdoor showers down at the beach: *We Want Fair Surfing Judges. NO TOMSON.* It made the newspapers and turned into this big ugly scene. After that, I knew I had to win on the international stage so that no one could ever accuse me or my family of cheating again. While Rabbit and I had very different upbringings, we both shared a burning desire to earn the respect of others. I remember Rabbit telling me that more than anything else he wanted to walk down the street of his hometown of Coolangatta as a surfer and get respect. That was a goal I could understand.

Awaiting a contest result. I obviously
wasn't happy with my performance.
Photograph by Dan Merkel.

Rabbit and I won contests in our separate countries then gravitated toward the ultimate proving ground on the North Shore in the winter of '75. There were other surfers with us, some of whom shared our dream: my cousin Michael Tomson, also from South Africa; and Australians Mark Richards, Ian Cairns, Peter Townend, Bruce Raymond, and Mark Warren. We battled against the Hawaiians, who were more famous than any of us. The year before, very few of us had managed to get invited to the major contests in Hawai'i, let alone win them. You have to understand how difficult it was to get an invitation. Out of twenty-four spots total in the Duke Kahanamoku contest, for example, only two were reserved for non-Hawaiians. That meant every other surfer in the world competed for those two slots.

SOMETiMES YOU ONLY NEED TO SAY iT TO YOURSELF TO MAKE A DREAM COME TRUE.

Once we got to the North Shore in '75, we set about making a name for ourselves by surfing the most famous beaches every day in the most dangerous conditions. People noticed when we paddled out at Sunset Beach and surfed huge, blown-out waves all day. They noticed when we tackled Pipeline and took off on waves that looked impossible to make. Rabbit and I fed off each other's energy and the energy of the surfers around us the entire season. Rabbit describes so well the mutual understanding the group of us shared:

> *I was excited about Shaun arriving in Hawai'i because somehow I knew that he was going to be one of my great rivals. I'd seen him at Bells and the Coke [contests in Australia] and I just knew, this was my guy. He loved tube-riding, we were the same age, and already you could see that he was a future superstar. I barely knew him but I liked him instantly. He was intelligent, articulate and I could sense that he was going to contribute to the fulfill-ment of my dream—that here was a surf star ready to win the hearts of the general public. He already had this aura about him, he was a bit aloof, he had the Hollywood looks—he was always going to be a sports star. I figured he was a guy I could run with and bounce off, we could be a foil for each other.*
>
> *It's weird thinking back on it—I barely knew Shaun at the time, or MR [Mark Richards] for that matter, we'd never discussed the dream of pro surfing as far as I can recall at that stage, but it was as if we all knew we had the same dream and we were going to help make it hap-pen together.*

Our commitment to radical surfing and to each other got us noticed. Not only did we get invited to the party that year, we took over the dance floor. Australians and South Africans placed first, second, and third in the three most famous contests, and we won four of them: I won the Pipeline Masters, Ian Cairns won the Duke Kahanamoku Invitational, and Mark Richards won the Smirnoff Pro-Am and the World Cup. Such domination of the Hawaiian events by outsiders has never happened before or since.

We also dominated the media coverage in the magazines: articles, photographs, even cover shots—I was featured on the covers of *Surfer* and *Surfing* (the two most popular surf magazines) in the same month that winter. We managed to transfer the radical maneuvers we did on smaller waves in our home countries to the huge waves of Hawai'i, and that made for exciting photographs in the magazines. We had new moves, a new attitude, and now that we'd caught everyone's attention, it was time to promote our ideas about a new future for surfing. It was the beginning of a cultural shift that kicked the old image of surfers as druggies and dropouts out the door and welcomed in a new era of the professional surfer. Almost forty years later, the World Championship Tour is thriving and surfers today make millions of dollars through contest winnings and sponsorship. Our vision of surfing got a huge push the day Rabbit and I stood at Ehukai Beach Park and looked out at the waves detonating off the second reef at Pipeline. We decided to paddle out, and the session is preserved in the final scene of Bill Delaney's *Free Ride,* a film that showcased the new generation of surfers who made their dreams come true through commitment and passion.

When Rabbit returned to Australia after our amazing surf season, he'd won a chunk of money in the contests and so filed his first tax return. At the bottom of that document he signed his name and added afterward "professional surfer." About a month later he received a letter from the government that read: "Dear Mr. Bartholomew, there is no such thing as a professional surfer." I suppose that bank manager in Coolangatta didn't agree, because the next time Rabbit walked into the bank and asked for a loan to buy a plane ticket to Hawai'i, he got the money.

As for me, I'd planned to return to the University of Natal after the '75 season and earn a law degree. It seemed a logical choice. I'd grown up in a Jewish household, and the expectations were that I would become a professional and follow the path of many of my friends—oftentimes it's easy to do what others expect of you rather than to pay attention to what you really enjoy doing and what you're good at. Rabbit's words on the beach that day in Hawai'i opened my eyes to other possibilities. He also challenged my competitive nature: he knew there was no way I was going to sit on the sidelines and watch him win contests and capture the title of world champion without a fight. Our teenage years are a time when we go through more rapid changes than at any other period in life, and it's no surprise that so many changes in the world come from the minds of young people. It's such an important time, a creative time, a time of endless possibilities. Forty years ago a group of teenagers dared to dream about a life of traveling around the world and getting paid to surf. And they made their dream come true for themselves and for so many others. So don't worry if someone doesn't have your dream listed in their little book. Go out there and write your own.

3.

I WILL FACE MY FEARS

I'm fifteen years old and sitting on the beach at Pipeline, wondering how I'm going to surf one of the most dangerous waves in the world. I'm staring out at an intimidating-looking swell—the biggest sets are double overhead—and I tell myself, "I'm gonna have to paddle out and have a go." I *want* to surf the wave—to test myself at a famous break under these conditions—but I don't know exactly how to go about it. How do you work up the courage to do something you've never done before?

I have a 6'6" board that surfers call a "mini-gun," shaped by a well-known Hawaiian surfer named Ben Aipa. I walk down to the water with that board tucked under my arm, and I start to paddle out. Unlike a lot of big-wave spots, Pipeline breaks fairly close to shore, so within a minute I'm stroking past the impact zone. I look to my left and watch a kneeboarder get sucked up the face of a wave and thrown over the falls into the sharp coral reef below. The wave is so incredibly steep, breaks with such raw power, that the only way to survive is to turn your back to the wave and paddle into the face with 100 percent commitment. Any hesitation at all and the wave will smash you into the reef.

I make it out to the lineup and wait for my wave. All these doubts are circling in my head: what if I wipe out like the knee-boarder? What if I crash into the reef? What if I drown? I try to shake the doubts because I know having them will distract me and I *will* fail.

But I can't shake them.

A wave peaks and swings in my direction. I know what I'm supposed to do, what I *want* to do, but how do I make myself do it? How do I face my fears?

⚊⚊⚊⚊⚊⚊

In 1967 my father took a trip to the United States and brought back the latest surf magazines for me and my younger brother, Paul. One of those issues reported that a Peruvian surfer—I still remember his name, Joaquín Miró Quesada—died by getting slammed into the reef on a ten-foot day at Pipeline. That marked the beginning of my dread for the spot and the knowledge that even a really good surfer, an experienced one, could easily die there. I also had a poster hanging above my bed of the Californian John Peck crouching backside at Pipeline, his hand grabbing the outside rail of the surfboard for balance. So I also knew the place could be surfed well by "regular footers"—guys like me and John Peck who rode with our left foot forward and so had our back to the wave, a much more dangerous position at Pipeline. The poster and surf magazine are just two examples of how famous Pipeline was and is, still today the wave where more surfers have died than any other break in the world. As a fifteen-year-old surfer from South Africa, a nobody in the lineup, I had to overcome the intimidating aura of a break that created two kinds of heroes: those who lived, like Peck, and those who died, like Quesada.

The reef is what gives the wave at Pipeline its beautiful cylindrical shape and makes it so dangerous. Surfers tell stories of getting parts of their bodies jammed into holes in the reef because of the force of the wave, which breaks in only a few feet of water. So many surfers have been injured there over the years. Oftentimes you'll see guys wear protective gear like helmets to protect themselves from bouncing off the reef. Certainly it's the bottom of the break that I have most in mind as I paddle into my first wave at Pipeline and it lifts me toward the sky.

But the locals are also on my mind because I don't want to embarrass myself in front of them. Pipeline has always attracted a tightly knit crew, surfers who live there and dedicate their entire lives to riding that one wave. The porches of the "Pipe houses," as they're called, are filled with locals who watch every session and pass out judgment. Visiting surfers have to pay their respects—and their dues—if they want to become accepted among the elite. Young surfers trying to make their mark aren't given many chances. Blow your first takeoff, and you won't be given a second. Guys will drop in on you, which only adds to the danger.

So the fame of Pipeline, the deadly reef, and the heavy locals are all crowding my mind as I stroke into that wave. How do I focus?

Here's what I do: I remind myself of what brought me to Pipeline in the first place. I'd been invited to compete in the Smirnoff Pro-Am, a surf contest held at Sunset Beach that year. I'd gotten the invitation by winning the junior division of the surfing championships in South Africa. I'd also made the quarterfinals of the World Amateur Championships in Australia that year and the final of a pro event in Durban—the Gunston 500. All that experience gives me confidence. "Do what you've

Banzai Pipeline, Hawai'i, November 1974. Taking the pink banana for its first test run shortly after taking a board across both shins at Sunset Beach. Photograph from the Tomson Collection.

done a thousand times before," I tell myself. "Stand up, drop down the face, and ride the wave to shore." I think about where I've succeeded before, and that gives me confidence for what lies ahead.

I rode my first wave at Pipeline that day. I didn't distinguish myself by any means, but I discovered something important about taking on challenges: the biggest obstacle I had to overcome that day was not the aura of Pipeline, the coral reef, or the local crew. It was myself. As soon as I convinced myself that I belonged, nothing could stop me.

Four years later, in 1974—the same winter I stayed at John's house in Pupukea—I'm back on the beach at Pipeline. My confidence has been shaken to the core by two things: a pink banana and a terrible wipeout at Sunset Beach.

First the wipeout.

I arrived in Hawai'i that year with a surfboard from my shaper in South Africa, Spider Murphy, made especially for big waves. The winter before, I'd stayed with Jeff Hakman, one of the top Hawaiian surfers of the era and also one of my heroes. Hakman had won all the prestigious events in the Islands—the Duke Kahanamoku Invitational at Sunset Beach (twice) and the Pipeline Masters. He had this beautiful big-wave gun made by a well-known shaper named Dick Brewer. At the time there was no better surfer, and no better shaper, to get a template from. So I took several pictures of the board and later gave them to Spider. I told him, "I want a board exactly like this." Any board good enough for Hakman was good enough for me.

Because surfboards are basically sculptures in foam, it's impossible to make an exact replica of another board if you're shaping by hand, especially from a set of photographs. Spider shaped the board for me, but it ended up not having as much curve along the bottom—what surfers call "rocker"—as Hakman's board. Without enough rocker, the nose of a surfboard will dig straight into the bottom of a wave on the drop, and the surfer will wipe out. At a place like Pipeline, this can mean the difference between life and death. I told Spider that Hakman's board had a lot more rocker toward the nose.

TRUST YOUR INSTINCTS, TRUST YOUR EXPERIENCE, FOCUS ON THE MOMENT, AND THE FEAR MIRACULOUSLY DISAPPEARS.

I had to leave for Hawai'i the next day, and since Spider had made the blank himself by pouring polyurethane into a concrete mold, he had to make do with the materials around the shop. He walked outside and grabbed a handful of bricks. He set my board down on a wooden rack, laminated fiberglass onto the foam core with resin, and as it dried he placed the bricks on the bottom deck and left them overnight. Basically he just bent more rocker into the board.

What could I say? When he was done, the board looked like it had a *lot* of curve to it, much more than Hakman's board, and in the wrong place, too. I didn't have enough time to get another board. I picked it up, ran my eyes over the deck and rails like I was really admiring his work. "Well," I said, "this looks good." I tucked it under my arm and left for the Islands. I would just have to make do.

It was my first session at Sunset Beach. I'd been invited again to surf in the Hang Ten Pro contest, so I wanted to get in a good practice session. I paddled my brand new Spider Murphy board right into the middle of the pack. The swell was up, all the locals and traveling pros were there, and I wanted to make a big impression.

And I did. The board was an absolute *dog*. Lack of rocker makes a board knife into the water; but too much rocker does the opposite: the board pushes water. All those bricks Spider had put on my board had turned it into a big banana. When I finally did catch a wave and made it to the bottom, some guy dropped straight in front of me and we collided: his board rammed into my shins so hard that I thought my legs were broken. I had to leave the water and go to the hospital, where they wrapped big bandages around them.

So I'm sitting on the beach at Pipeline. The bandages have come off but I'm still smarting from the wipeout and the knowledge that my board didn't work at all in those waves. I did have another board with me. A company called Lightning Bolt had begun giving up-and-coming surfers free boards to help promote their name. Barry Kanaiaupuni, a fantastic surfer and well-known shaper on the North Shore, had made me a great board. But I didn't want to use his board that day because if I broke it—and this was common at Pipeline—I wouldn't have a board for the upcoming contest at Sunset Beach.

So the swell is up at Pipe, and I need to practice. I have my Spider Murphy board. It's a real dog, but what choice do I have? I know the board paddles slowly and pushes water; there's a strong possibility that it will hang me up in the worst possible

place on the wave—right at the top in the lip—and that the wave will launch me headfirst down into the reef. As I sit considering all this—debating whether it might be better to wait for a smaller day, or until I have more experience on the board, or perhaps until the crowd thins and the photographers pack their gear—the heckling starts from the Pipe houses: "Hey, Shaun," someone yells. "Where you going with that pink banana?"

The Spider Murphy board was supposed to be blood red, the color of the classic Pipeline big-wave gun. But the paint job hadn't come out right, and it turned out pink. And with all the rocker bent into the nose—a pink banana.

Hearing that comment from the Pipe houses reminds me of the first time I surfed Pipeline four years earlier, all those doubts crowding my head. The recent wipeout at Sunset and my ankle injury, my lack of confidence in the pink board, and the heckling all make me doubt myself. There's even more pressure this time around because I'm older and better known: people have higher expectations, and that's partly the reason for the heckling from the Pipe houses. I know it's done in good fun, but it rattles me.

Sometimes it's easy to let other peoples' doubts become your own, to let them prevent you from taking on a challenging situation. I decide to forget about the pink board and my wipeout at Sunset. I block everything from my mind except trusting the experience that has gotten me back to Pipeline, and I grab my board and paddle out.

When my wave finally comes, I spin around and stroke hard into the face with absolute focus and commitment. I feel the sudden lift skyward and jump immediately to my feet, pushing myself over the edge toward the coral reef.

And then something magical happens: because of the extreme rocker, the board slots perfectly into the face. And I

The extreme curve of the pink banana allowed me to fit into previously unridden parts of the wave. Banzai Pipeline, 1975. Photograph by Lance Trout.

mean perfectly. I drop down, turn as hard and as fast as I can, and the board holds tight because the bottom, with all that extreme curve, fits hand-in-glove with the equally extreme angle of the breaking wave.

The rest of the ride really is history. I ride that board for the next five seasons at Pipeline and never wipe out on the drop. I win the Pipeline Masters the following year, and the world title two years later. Most importantly, I'm able to do what every major design innovation in surfing has accomplished over the past century: open up new spaces on the wave. Suddenly I have equipment that will take me to places on the wave that I have previously only imagined, and this gives me an enormous boost of confidence.

I was tremendously lucky because of the design fluke. But I was only able to take advantage of that luck after working through doubts and fears that could have kept me on the beach. I would never have gone on to win the Pipeline Masters, or to surf at the highest level of my life in those years from 1974 to 1978, if I hadn't worked up the nerve to take off on that first wave at Pipeline when I was fifteen years old, or if I hadn't ignored those voices from the Pipe houses when I was nineteen. I relied instead on the voices that come from within: trust your instincts, trust your experience, focus on the moment, and the fear miraculously disappears.

4.

I WILL NEVER GIVE UP

It's 1975 and I'm twenty years old. I've wiped out on the biggest wave of my life during the finals of a contest—the Smirnoff Pro. Fans pack the beach and line the cliffs surrounding Waimea Bay, on the North Shore of Oʻahu in Hawaiʻi. Television cameras on shore capture every ride and every wipeout for all the viewers sitting in their living rooms.

The first thing I do when I break the surface is look for my surfboard. We didn't use leashes back then. We didn't have Jet Skis as surfers do today that race out and rescue you, haul you back to safety. I see my board floating a hundred yards away in a deep spot twenty-five yards from shore. The wave at Waimea breaks a few hundred yards out, then backs off over deep water before reforming into ferocious shorepound. I think my back is broken, but I need to get to my board. I can hardly move my legs. I'm disoriented from lack of oxygen and the pounding my body has taken.

Waimea Bay, O'ahu. At that time, the Mount Everest of surfing and the site of my most harrowing wipeout. Photograph by Dan Merkel.

I start swimming toward the beach—slowly at first, then more desperately, constantly looking over my shoulder to see if any more waves are coming. I'm also worried about the fast-moving riptide that could suck me out to sea.

I reach my board and drag myself onto the deck. I look first to the beach—twenty seconds of paddling and I'll be safe on the sand. I look back to the lineup: the contest is still running, and guys are scrambling out of the way as another wave explodes off the reef. I just experienced the worst wipeout of my life, and I know I cannot survive another like it. My confidence is shaken to the core—who I am, and what I believe I can do. The decision I make that moment—to paddle in or paddle out—is a turning point in my life.

ΙΛΙΛΙΛΙΛΙΛΙΛΙΛ

Looking back I see that I didn't put myself in a position to succeed that day. For starters, I'd never surfed Waimea Bay. The place needs a giant swell to work, and oftentimes weeks or months can go by without a ripple. So I had not expected to ride Waimea at all that winter. Second, I didn't even own a board big enough to ride waves that size, so I had to borrow one for the contest. It was a recipe for disaster: my first time out at the most challenging big-wave break in the world, and I was using a board I'd never surfed on. Imagine Tiger Woods or Phil Mickelson breaking in a brand-new driver—no practice shots on the driving range—during the final day of the Masters. The only difference is that a wayward slice wouldn't cost the golfers their lives. At Waimea Bay this was a real possibility.

I knew this, of course, but I was young and fired up: money, reputation, personal pride, professional stature—all of these were on the line. Waimea Bay was the Mount Everest of surfing, and if I didn't scale its summit, my reputation would never rank among the very best. So I put that borrowed board under my arm and paddled out.

The first wave I stroked into was pushing twenty feet, definitely a solid size. I'd wanted to pick off the very first one that came through to shake off the nervous energy, get used to how the wave broke, and most importantly find out if the board actually worked for me. I'd taken a calculated risk and paddled farther to the inside than the other competitors. It turned out my calculations were off. Way off. I'd focused too much on getting that first wave. Not knowing the break at all, I didn't realize that I'd placed myself in a very dangerous situation.

I remember catching the wave and standing up cleanly. As I dropped down the face I thought, *Well, this is pretty easy.* I was a quarter way down, knees bent, arms straight out in perfect balance.

THE DECISION I MAKE THAT MOMENT—TO PADDLE IN OR PADDLE OUT—IS A TURNING POINT IN MY LIFE.

The wave hit the shallow part of the reef and jacked up. The face went absolutely vertical. The board came completely out of the water, and I began free-falling with my arms and legs windmilling out of control. The board hit the bottom first, then I landed on the board and bounced off with so much force that my body began skipping across the surface of the water. Normally water is a soft cushion; at high speeds, though, it feels like asphalt.

The worst thing that can happen to a surfer who wipes out in big waves is staying on the surface. It's critical to try and penetrate, or else the wave can land directly on top of you. Even getting sucked up the face and going over the falls with the white water—as gut-wrenching as that experience can be—is preferable to having the entire wave hit you squarely. When this happens a surfer can easily be knocked unconscious and drown. The lifeguards at Waimea are the best in the world, but even for them a rescue in the impact zone is very tricky. Donnie Solomon, a twenty-five-year-old surfer from California, died in 1995 after trying to paddle through a set wave at the Bay. There was simply not enough time to save him once he went under.

That wave did hit me squarely. I felt like I'd been walking along the highway and gotten hammered by a truck from behind. A terrifying impact. Never to this day have I been struck so hard by a wave. It was a feeling of absolute crushing violence, an unbelievable sensation of force and power. I couldn't have imagined any human body taking such a beating and surviving.

The wave plunged me into blackness. I've never been especially conscious of hearing noise underwater, but as I was being driven to the depths, I heard horrifying sounds coming from above as the wave pounded across the Bay.

So there I am floating on my board after the wipeout; I'm looking from sea to shore, wondering which direction to take. The consequences of that moment have meant everything to my career; at the time I didn't even have a career in surfing since the World Tour didn't begin until the following year. And yet for all of its importance, the action itself was so simple: I swung my board around and paddled back out.

Australian Mark Richards went on to win the contest. I rode a few more waves in my heat—all smaller than the one I'd wiped out on. Waimea taught me a critical lesson about preparation and perseverance. Never again will I make the mistakes I did that day. Although I didn't give myself the best chance to succeed, I laid the foundation for future success by taking those strokes back to the lineup. I knew after my wipeout that I was essentially done for the contest. But I told myself that I didn't have to win—didn't even have to surf my best during the rest of the heat. It was enough to turn my board around and face those waves again.

ΛΥΛΥΛΥΛΥΛΥΛΥΛ

If anyone had told me while I was getting smashed by that wave at Waimea that the business world would be a *lot* harder than surfing, I never would've believed them. But after retiring from the tour in 1990 I had two devastating free falls in business, both of which shook my confidence even more than the Bay. And yet the knowledge that I hadn't given up on myself that day has carried me through each crisis.

The first occurred in 1995. I was sitting in the waiting room of a well-known surf clothing company in Southern California. It had not been my first interview for a job. Not even my second. I'd arrived that week heavily in debt after having closed the doors on my own clothing company in South Africa, and I was looking for a job. The consequences of going under at that point extended beyond my own survival to that of my wife, Carla, and my five-year-old son, Mathew. After an excellent career on the World Tour as a champion surfer, as the owner of a successful clothing company that had sponsored other surfers, as someone who'd always been optimistic and successful, I sat in that chair and realized that people had very little interest in Shaun Tomson. Suddenly I was no longer a success. I was an ex–pro surfer looking for a job that no one wanted to give me.

After the interview I was very shaken, not unlike the feelings I'd experienced after my wipeout at Waimea, but more on an emotional level. I had a similar life-changing decision to make, but this time I understood, as I hadn't before, how serious the consequences of that decision would be for my family's future. And yet it would've been easier to get on a plane and go back to my wife and son in South Africa rather than face another interview and risk those terrible blows to my ego.

I phoned Carla. Her advice to me was simple: *Keep looking for a job.* She knew—for the sake of my own self-confidence— that I had to stay out there and keep trying. She was right, and I needed to have that reaffirmation from someone so important in my life.

I did paddle back out and find a job with a great clothing company, Patagonia. Yvon Chouinard and his wife, Malinda, offered me a great position, as did my old friend Pat O'Neill at O'Neill Wetsuits. I eventually settled down with Patagonia. They were wonderful to me and brought out my entire family from South Africa. All the good things they say about that great company are true, and working for the Chouinards was both challenging and inspiring. After a couple of years with Patagonia I spent some time at O'Neill Wetsuits, but ultimately Carla and I decided to start our own company again, this time in Santa Barbara, California. We knocked on doors, talked about our ideas, and raised over a million dollars in funding. The clothing business is very demanding, and we couldn't have worked harder. Carla designed all the clothing while I oversaw the day-to-day business operations and directed sales and production.

After three years we had built up a great product line with hundreds of stores from California to New York, dealing with some of the best department stores in the nation: Nordstrom, Saks Fifth Avenue, Barneys, and Bloomingdale's. And then 9/11 hit, and the bottom fell out again.

Our company, Solitude, experienced what many businesses did after the terrorist attacks: sales plummeted but overheads didn't, and ultimately we had a hard time finding investors to recapitalize. Clothing is an especially expensive product to fund, with a great outlay of time and money on the front end (to make the clothing), and the possibility of very little return due to changing trends, or even an event as unforeseen as the attacks on the Twin Towers. To make a long story short, I was looking at my second business failing in less than ten years. We didn't have enough cash to fund our next season, and investors were holding onto their money until the political and economic situation stabilized.

On a Monday we began clearing out our offices in Santa Barbara: furniture, inventory, employees. During that week everything went except four things: my desk, my telephone, my computer, and our company's server. I had no idea what I was going to do, but as long as I had a phone hooked up I could still make calls.

Turned out I didn't have to. By chance, one of my best pals, Herk Clark, met a man named Randy Paskal at a little league baseball game that Herk was coaching the next day, Saturday. They got to talking, and Randy said he admired Herk's shirt. How many times does that happen? One guy telling another that he likes his shirt! Herk mentioned it was a Solitude shirt, and that we were unfortunately in the throes of closing up shop. Randy mentioned that he was familiar with the brand, and that he and his father, Joe, invested in a number of businesses and would like to meet us.

I met the Paskals the next day, Sunday. Monday morning we started moving everything back into our offices and a few years later we sold Solitude to Oxford Industries, a publicly traded company on the New York Stock Exchange. What is it they say in baseball? *It ain't over till it's over.*

I'm still in the clothing business and face more competition now than I ever did in surf contests. I've certainly gotten my fair share of poundings, too. But I've always made it back up with the help of family and friends. Whatever comes over the horizon at me, I draw strength from knowing that my experience in the water supports other aspects of my life that now take priority. I may get worked over again in the clothing business and start looking for a safe place on the beach. But my confidence comes more from working toward my goals rather than the goal itself. Goals are temporary; my sense of self-worth—the kind of person I want to be—stays with me the rest of my life. If there's a challenge out there to meet, you know which direction I'll be headed: back out there to catch another wave.

5.

I WILL CREATE

Back in the '80s I was based in Los Angeles while competing on the pro surfing tour. During one of my brief stopovers I got a call from a producer at one of the large film studios about a "top secret project." I ended up sitting across the table from a prosperous-looking guy in an Italian suit on the backlot of Universal Studios. His name was Cubby Broccoli—a Hollywood heavyweight who'd produced all of the James Bond movies. Broccoli and his director, John Glen, had invited me out for lunch. I knew I wasn't cut out to be the new Bond so I couldn't figure out their angle.

It turned out the Hollywood crew definitely wasn't looking for me to be the new James Bond. They were interested in tubes. They had this idea for a plotline in their next film, and they'd heard that I'd built a reputation for being one of the best guys riding deep inside a tube.

"What do you call it?" they asked me. "The tunnel right inside the wave where you're invisible? Could you double for Bond and find a wave that he could ride for a long time inside the tunnel in secret, and then get safely to the beach where the guards in the machine gun nests on the cliff couldn't see him?"

They wanted a big, high-powered opening scene that a mainstream audience hadn't experienced before. They wanted to reveal that secret world known only to surfers. They thought it would be exciting, dramatic, heart stopping—all the things we'd expect from the beginning of a Bond movie. It was a creative idea, and they'd come to the right guy. I'm always interested in promoting surfing to mainstream audiences. Riding inside the tube is a creative act in itself, one that I revolutionized in the '70s by imagining a better way to maneuver my surfboard on the face of the wave. I'm no James Bond, and this isn't top secret information, but it's exciting to know that each of us has the ability to create something new that will influence the lives of people around us in a positive way. And you don't have to be a secret agent to do it.

ʔʌʔʌʔʌʔʌʔʌʔʌ

Those producers were right: riding inside a tube is exciting and dramatic. It's a very special place and only relatively few people know about it. Surfers mainly. Surfers have been riding inside of tubes on a regular basis since the 1960s, but the maneuver really came into its own in the late '60s and early '70s with the invention of the shortboard. Before that there were guys like Conrad Canha at Ala Moana (a break near Waikīkī) who could ride in the tube on a regular basis, but the surfboards at that time were big and heavy, mostly designed to ride out in front of the curl rather than deep inside of it.

As boards got shorter, lighter, and more maneuverable, surfers began to explore the inside of waves. A spot like Pipeline, on the North Shore of O'ahu, became the most famous wave in the world because of its dramatic and dangerous tubes. More surfers have died at Pipe than at any other surf spot in the world—a dozen or so over the years—so it's a place that offers the greatest reward because it involves the ultimate risk.

EACH OF US HAS THE ABILITY TO CREATE SOMETHING NEW THAT WILL INFLUENCE THE LIVES OF PEOPLE AROUND US IN A POSITIVE WAY.

But for every surfer who has died at Pipe, hundreds have gotten the ride of their lives. Up through the mid-'70s, the best surfers—guys like Hawaiians Gerry Lopez and Rory Russell—drew very clean lines inside the tube; either standing or crouching, they usually found a track and stayed on it until the compression building up inside the breaking wave blew them

Time may be slowed down inside the tube, but a wipeout on the unpredictable inside section at Sunset Beach can happen suddenly and unexpectedly. Photograph by Dan Merkel.

out the end in a glorious cloud of spray. Even with the amazing acrobatic airs surfers are boosting over waves these days, and the extremes of tow-in surfing at remote outer reefs, riding inside the tube remains the most intense sensation in our sport and its definitive maneuver.

I loved getting tubed growing up in my hometown of Durban. I surfed regularly at the Bay of Plenty, which offers a great variety of waves, including long and hollow tube rides. I had posters on my bedroom wall of Hawaiian surfers getting tubed at Pipeline; these guys were my heroes, but there was something inside of me—a creative impulse is the best way to describe it—that wasn't satisfied with simply staying on one track and letting the wave dictate my path through its insides. I wanted to create my own path. The tracks I had in mind were not straight the way a train runs but serpentine: my board weaving inside the tube as the wave rolled through its erratic motion. No two waves break exactly the same way, so why should I expect to stay in one position and make it through on a regular basis? I needed to adapt my motion to a medium that was constantly shifting. I needed to match Pipeline's progressive curve with an equally progressive style. I can't say that I had an image set in my mind of how I was going to surf; rather I had an impulse to be active inside of the wave rather than stationary, and I opened my mind to possibilities that my body eventually explored through feeling and instinct.

I've already mentioned my first experience at Pipeline in Chapter 3, and the many benefits of riding Spider Murphy's board, which gave me a tremendous technical advantage because I could take off later and ride farther back inside the tube. But to reap the benefits of that board I first had to envision the possibility of moving inside the wave.

The average tube ride is short—maybe three or four seconds—but the great ones linger in your memory for life. At Pipeline the first thing you have to do is stroke over the edge of the wave, fight past the unrelenting crowd and the trade winds clutching at you—sometimes blinding you by blowing spray in your eyes—and survive the serrated chops twisting up the face that can buckle your knees and launch you off the board. More than anything you fight past the fear that this takeoff will be your last. Pipeline has an impact zone of death, a sharp coral bottom littered with crevasses and caves. As soon as you drop down and look over your shoulder—if you ride with your left foot forward like me, that's what you have to do at Pipe—you start looking for that sandy spot at the end of the ride.

The first thing you notice after the wave throws over you is the absence of sound, the utter silence. A tube is the quietest place on the planet. There's all kinds of noise surrounding you—water crashing, wind blowing, foam surging—but you don't hear a thing.

Then there's the time distortion. At high speeds in the tube, you experience the sensation of the wave moving in slow motion. The body is reacting to danger. When you can't fight and you can't run, your senses go to red alert: every nerve becomes a seismograph, registering and reacting to the slightest shift in the immediate environment. In this altered, hypersensitive state of mind and body, the wave actually appears to break in slow motion. The result is that you feel like you have all the time in the world to react: adjust your stance, dodge the lip, shift your weight forward or backward, carve up and down the wall, anything that allows you to move forward and keep from getting crushed. The tube is the most dangerous place to be on a wave. One mistake, and the breaking wave will either drive you directly to the bottom—often covered in razor-sharp reef—or suck you up the face first and then drive you to the bottom. There's no escape. A couple of years ago at Pipe, I got trapped inside a tube—caught by the white water rushing up the face behind the tail of my board—and in a moment I was slammed into the reef on my back. While I was pinned to the bottom, my board smashed into my face and broke my nose. At Pipe, that's called getting off lucky.

Spots like Pipeline that have the most intense tubes also have the worst bottoms: jagged lumps of coral—those harsh obstacles of pain for surfers—that sometimes form into dangerous caves.

Caves are the worst. Sometimes surfers get forced into them, wedged down there until they drown. Back in Durban there's a short and intense wave called Cave Rock that rears up over a very shallow reef. On one particularly vicious wipeout, the wave threw me into the rocky bottom feet first and straight into a cave, my hands pinned to my sides. There I was beneath the roiling wave, totally jammed into a hole, unable to move or even struggle—only my head stuck out of the reef six feet beneath the surface. I had a brief moment of absolute panic, and then the wave pounded me again and ripped me right out of the hole.

There's no better sensation in surfing than riding twenty feet back in your own secret world, invisible from shore, hidden by a thundering sheet of exploding white water. And you're in complete control—at least sometimes it feels that way.

Here's the thing: my ability to maneuver inside of the tube didn't come while I was sitting on the beach thinking about it, or floating in the lineup waiting for the perfect wave to swing my way. It happened while I was actually inside of the wave. In order to create, you have to be in motion—physically or mentally striving toward a goal. Only then will new possibilities open for you. For me that place is a tube: a space where my sensations are sharpened, the immediacy of life brought into focus, and all that matters is to experience the fullness of that moment to the best of my ability. To create that moment for myself. There were times when I believed I could actually control the wave breaking around me. It was an illusion, of course, but I felt like I could curve that wall to my will. It's a magical moment, an incredible moment, generated by an intense synchronicity with my environment. Imagine feeling the simultaneous need to escape a dangerous situation and yet linger so you can burn every pixel of that moment into your memory. Open your mind and body to creative possibilities, and these moments will happen for you, too.

And you will inspire others. The progressive lines I drew inside the tube in the mid-'70s got me noticed, especially when I started winning contests. Other surfers saw how effective my techniques were for getting through the tube—at prolonging my ride, really, which is what every surfer in the world wants to do, professional or not. And those surfers drew on their own particular strengths and creativity, which brought more innovation to surfing. Today surfers do such incredible maneuvers while riding inside the tube—both frontside and backside. They can get tubed at will and stay inside for ten seconds and more; they ride on the foam ball—that cushion of air and water that cyclones deep inside a tube—with the kind of balance and control few would have thought possible in my era. Yes, surfers today have better equipment. But they've also been inspired by seeing how surfers who came before them opened up new spaces on the wave. This encourages them to do the same. They will inspire a new generation to go beyond them and explore parts of the wave that today appear inaccessible. We have a fundamental human urge to create and to leave a legacy that will make the world a better place for those who come after us. Every time you take the opportunity to create—no matter how brief—you give the world one more reason to grow and to be inspired.

6.

I WILL HEAL

My father, Ernest "Chony" Tomson, was one of South Africa's most promising swimmers. In 1946, at the age of twenty-two, he was training to hopefully represent South Africa in the 1948 Olympic Games. One day while he was out surfing at a place called South Beach—just having fun riding waves on a little wooden board we called a dumper board—a Zambezi shark attacked him. It hit him so hard that his entire body flew out of the water. When he landed he was missing most of the muscle on his upper right arm.

He later told me that he'd never seen the ocean clear so fast. Men scrambled up the pilings of the nearby pier, shredding their hands and chests on the sharp mussel shells. With all the confusion and the blood, people on the beach at first thought there'd been multiple attacks. One swimmer, Brian Biljoen, managed to keep his head in the chaos, and he pulled my father into shore. They rushed him to Addington Hospital on the beachfront, and the doctors immediately packed his arm in ice. Luckily it was high summer and all the beach hotels had laid in their store of ice for the tourists.

My father endured multiple operations over the next few months, including painful skin grafts from his stomach that left deep scars, but he never regained the use of his right arm. He didn't like to talk about the attack. If one of us kids—my younger brother Paul or my sister Tracy—ever asked him about it, he'd always answer with a joke. *The shark died of blood poisoning,* he'd tell us with a laugh. Or, *I don't know who got the bigger shock, me or the shark.* My mother later told me that he experienced terrible nightmares. But because of his sense of humor, we thought him totally unselfconscious of the terrible scars the shark had left on his body. I never considered him disabled in any way, but his arm steadily withered from lack of use, and his right fist remained in a permanent clinch.

Imagine my father in 1946: a young man with a tremendous swimming career ahead of him now unable to do what he most loved, and reminded of that fact every time he looked down at an arm he couldn't move and a hand he couldn't open. He had every right to be bitter about the experience and to turn his back on the ocean.

And yet some of my earliest memories are of my father taking me by the hand and leading me down into the water at North Beach, a spot three hundred yards from where the shark attack had nearly ended his life. Love for the ocean helped heal his spirit, and he instilled that love in me from a very young age.

ᴧᴠᴧᴠᴧᴠᴧᴠᴧ

When I was growing up we used to call going for a swim *going for a Tiger Tim,* or just a *Tiger* for short. I'd say to my father, *C'mon, let's go for a Tiger, let's go for a Tiger.* I was six or seven years old. I remember him holding my hand and walking me down to the water. He spoke in a rhyming slang, inherited from the Cockneys in England who'd emigrated to South Africa and brought their particular way of speaking with them. So we didn't say money, we said *Tom Funny*. Sharks were called *Johnny Darks,* or simply *Johnnys.* When someone disappeared in the ocean we'd say, *A Johnny took 'em,* or, *They got hit by a Johnny.*

In South Africa during the summertime heavy rains caused the Umgeni River to swell, and red silt washed down to the ocean and clouded the water. So it was very hard to see beneath the surface. Also in the summertime a northeasterly wind blew down from the Mozambique Channel, and big jellyfish floated in with their long, painful stingers. And of course there were always the *Johnnys* lurking about.

Imagine a man profoundly aware of the dangers of the ocean—himself savaged by a shark that destroyed his swimming career—and yet here he was placing his first-born son, whom he loved deeply, straight out there in the ocean and being enthusiastic about it, and loving about it, and teaching me how to swim, and teaching me how to bodysurf, and loving the fact that I enjoyed a career where I spent most every day in the ocean. And his enthusiasm radiated out to the whole surfing community, especially in Durban. He sponsored a great number of young guys to encourage them to keep surfing, and he watched us all the time with binoculars to see who was surfing well, and to offer advice. And he did it all in a very special way so that we wanted to do well both for him and for our own sakes. He was never overbearing about it. He understood that competition was important, but he made us keep the idea of winning in perspective because he wanted us to have a great time doing it. For him, sports competition was one area where people could get on together and interact with one another in an honorable way.

I had a chance to experience my father's faith in competition in the days following his death. It was 1981 and I was in Australia for the beginning of the World Tour. The year before I'd placed third—my best finish since winning the title in 1977. So things were going very well for me. I had every reason to believe they'd get even better. It was the opening of a new season, and I had my sights set on another world title.

Then my father had a heart attack. I got the call from my mother in South Africa. And for the first time in my life, I completely lost all motivation to surf: not just to compete, but even to paddle out. My father and I had been super close. He'd been the number one motivating force in my life: my coach since I was a kid, my biggest fan, my inspiration. He'd been present for every heat along the way, from my first victory in South Africa to my world title. Even afterward he continued to advise me on surfing equipment, my career, everything. I'd been keen to surf for as long as I could remember, but after he passed away I hardly even wanted to look at a wave.

Around this same time Australian surfer Simon Anderson came out with a brand-new board—the three-finned thruster—which has gone on to become the most popular design in the history of surfing. When I saw Simon's board, I thought, *If there's a new trend starting up, I want to be ready to jump right in.* But I also felt conflicted: I had moments of deep sadness for the loss of my father, yet I knew he would have advised me to keep competing. Days would go by where I had no desire to see the beach, and yet at the same time I was intrigued by the possibilities of Simon's board and the chance perhaps to regain my standing as world champion. And there were actually days when I woke up and wanted to go surfing and to win, and then I'd feel bad about my enthusiasm. As if somehow it were disrespectful to the memory of my father.

So those were some of the mixed emotions I was experiencing. When I'd first seen Simon on the beach with his board, I said to myself, *Well, this design looks pretty good.* And our brief conversation went something like this:

"Is it a good board, then?"

"Three weeks, mate," Simon said. "Three weeks, and you'll be riding one." And he laughed. That is how confident he was.

"Well," I said, "you're most probably right."

I'd said it half jokingly because Simon has a great sense of humor. He'd not yet won any contests on the board, so I was interested but obviously not convinced.

Well, it didn't take long. Simon won the next two events in Australia and was ranked number one in the world—he'd actually beat me in the final of the second event. Afterward I phoned him up and told him very directly, "Simon, I'd love to get one of those boards."

Now here you have a situation where a guy is the top-ranked surfer in the world. And he's come out with a fantastic new design that'd won him two contests right off the bat. He could have simply said no and hung up on me. I was one of Simon's biggest rivals. At the time I was rated number three or four in the world. We would compete against each other for the title the rest of the year: in South Africa, in Japan, in California, in France, and in the final events in the Hawaiian Islands.

Simon knew I was going through a rough period after my dad died. Still, he could have let me down easy: "I'm sorry, Shaun. I'm keeping this for myself." I would not have thought any less of him, and he certainly would have been completely within his rights.

You know what he told me? "Okay." And he shaped me two thrusters just like that, and he gave them to me. Simon comes from a long tradition of great surfers who are also terrific shapers, and so it was the shaper in Simon who basically

A shark bite destroyed my father's swimming career, but he totally supported me in my competitive surfing aspirations. In 1970, at age 14, I made the South African surfing team and he was a proud Dad. Newspaper articles from the *Daily News*. Photographs from the Tomson Collection.

DURBAN SWIMMER'S OWN STORY OF SHARK ATTACK

I Was Lifted Clear From The Water

In this article Ernest Tomson, Natal's 220 yards swimming champion, who is also a Durban lifesaver, tells the story of the attack made on him last month by a large shark at the South Beach.

He is one of the few South Africans to escape a shark attack with his life, although he was seriously injured and in grave danger for some time. He is now recovering from his injuries at Addington Hospital and may soon be discharged.

By Ernest Tomson

IT was an ideal day for surfing—and for sharks. The tide was running full and a bunch of us were about a hundred yards out waiting for slides.

A beauty came up and I caught it with my surfboard. The others missed and I came to alone right through the surf in the water's edge. It was getting late, but I decided to go in again for one more slide. I began swimming out with my board to my right hand. About 15 yards behind me were two other swimmers.

Suddenly, I felt something come shooting underneath me. For a moment I thought it was a friend trying to catch my leg.

And then I felt my shoulder in a vicious grip. The terrific speed at which the shark was travelling lifted me bodily from the water. My right arm was flung out and it seemed as if it had been torn from its socket. The surfboard was buried some yards away.

Then I saw the shark leap out of the water. It was about the size of a man.

Panic - Stricken

At first I was absolutely panic-stricken. I started shouting loudly and kicked my legs. I was worried that it would attack again.

By this time my wound had left a long trail of blood which I thought would attract any attacker or other sharks in the vicinity. If which I am sure there were quite a few. I resigned myself to my fate.

The two swimmers behind me were swimming furiously for the shore and a terrible feeling of loneliness came over me. I turned over on my back, put up my left arm and started kicking back for the shore. It seemed miles away.

Looking shoreward, I saw one of the swimmers coming back for me. It was Brian Biljoen, who held me up and gave me encouragement until the professional life-saver, Wally Power, came out with a line.

Still Conscious

By this time I was weak, but still very conscious. The waves were very big near the shore and as they broke we were swamped. By this time I had lost a great deal of blood and was finding it difficult to breathe.

I was then brought to the beach by the lifesavers who had a stretcher ready. They rushed me to the ambulance and I remember telling them to hurry as I thought I would not live to see another day.

The lifesavers were really magnificent and to them I owe my life. Such was their swiftness and coolness that I reached hospital in 10 minutes.

The big lift in the hospital would not work as the lifesavers ran me up two flights of stairs. The hospital staff was ready and I had immediate blood transfusions and my arm was packed in ice.

While waiting for the anaesthetic to take effect a young nurse kept her hand immersed in the ice to stop the flow of blood from my arm. I was then wheeled to the theatre.

thought: *This is a new design. It's working great for me, and I've won two contests in a row. Other surfers need to ride this board.* It's the kind of sportsmanship my father championed his whole life, and in the days following his death, Simon's generosity helped me work through the complicated feelings I had.

LOVE FOR THE OCEAN HELPED HEAL MY FATHER'S SPIRIT, AND HE INSTILLED THAT LOVE IN ME FROM A VERY YOUNG AGE.

I still miss my father every day. I used to phone him after every event, often telling him that I'd not done so well then busting him up with the news that I'd won. It was a joke we liked to share and one that I'd learned from him. I'll never forget the first time he pulled it on me in the Gunston 500 in South Africa. He was acting as a spotter during the contest: he would stand in the judges' tower and call off the colors of the jerseys as the surfers stood up, to assist the judges in their scoring. In 1973 I was standing on the presentation stage with five other finalists. I could see my father sitting up in the judges' tower about twenty yards away, and I knew he could see the scores. It'd been a very close final. At one point I looked up at him for some form of assurance. I remember him slowly shaking his head at me, subtly giving me the thumbs down. I was devastated. When the results were announced minutes later, I'd won! He'd known all along, of course, but he couldn't let a great opportunity for a joke slip by. It was my first victory in a professional contest, one of many that we enjoyed together.

I remember the phone call I got from my mother after he died. She told me simply that he was gone. No warning, no time for me to prepare, just my mother on the other end saying how terribly sorry she was. I think she'd never stopped loving him even though they'd divorced many years before. A son measures his own mortality by his parents. I was young, strong, invincible, had never even contemplated death. After the previous event— where I'd placed fifth—I hadn't phoned my father as I normally did. I hadn't wanted to talk about my poor performance. I didn't even have the chance to say goodbye to him.

Each person has a different approach to overcoming tragedy. For me, I'll always think about my father and the way he embraced the ocean throughout his life and the lives of his children. His courage is one of the reasons why I visit schools and clubs today and tell the story of my son, Mathew: partly to heal myself, and partly to share stories with others who may also need to heal.

7.

I WILL PRAY

During World War II, my mother, Marie, lived on Malta, a small island in the Mediterranean Sea that sits between Italy and North Africa. When Italy joined the war on the side of Germany in 1940, Malta became their first target because it was a British colony and a heavily used port for ships transferring soldiers and supplies to Europe and North Africa. The island eventually became one of the most heavily bombed places in history, enduring more than three thousand air raids over two years. During one six-week period in 1942, fifteen million pounds of bombs were dropped on the island.

My mother—she was a young girl at the time—lived with two older siblings and her mother in a two-story house built on a big rock in the city of Senglea. They were so close to the harbor that sailors from moored ships could wave to the family as they sat on the veranda. My mother and her brother, Terence, could fish right from the first story of the house using a stick of bamboo

My mom Marie, sister Tracy, and brother Paul with me on the beach in Durban. My earliest memories are of spending time with my family on the beach where I eventually started surfing. My mom is only fifteen years away from her childhood on Malta and over three thousand Italian and German bombing raids. Photograph from the Tomson Collection.

and a string. An English couple also lived near them, in a house a bit farther away from the sea. After the air raids started—first by the Italians, then the Germans—Marie's mother went over to them and knocked on their door. "If the air raids get worse," she told them, "please come down into the boathouse with us and you'll be safe."

That couple shut the door in her face.

Marie's mother—my grandmother—was a very social person. She sang and played the piano and loved having people over to her house. When war was declared in 1939, she was in England with Marie and my uncle Terence. She traveled overland through France, Switzerland, and Italy to get back to Malta so the family could all be together again. Her husband—my grandfather—had originally taken a job on Malta as an engineer in 1936 because there was a depression happening in England and he got this great opportunity to work in the colony. Marie was six years old at the time. They all loved Malta; it was a beautiful island with wonderful weather, and so different from England, which has a cold and damp climate much of the year. Marie's mother hated the cold. The beaches of Malta are among the most beautiful in the world, with that deep blue water typical of the Mediterranean region. Like my grandmother, my grandfather was very friendly. He died before the war with Italy, in 1940, and was so loved by the locals that instead of having his body transported to the cemetery in a hearse, a group of Englishmen carried the casket halfway, and then a group of Maltese men carried it the rest of the way. After that it was just my grandmother, Marie, and her brother, Terence. Marie's older sister got married to a captain of a minesweeper and during the war ended up working for Britain's Decoding Office, trying to break enemy codes.

That English couple was never friendly to Marie's family. They didn't socialize at all. They often scoffed at my mother's spirituality during the air raids. "Your mum says pray," they'd tell Marie. "We don't believe in that at all." Instead of going to a nearby boathouse with Marie's family and other neighbors during the air raids, they chose to wait out the bombing in the stairwell of their house. There was a lot of praying going on in that boathouse—not much else to do with bombs dropping out of the sky—and perhaps the couple felt uncomfortable being around people who showed such strong religious devotion.

The boathouse was close to Marie's house and built out of stone, so it was much safer than a wooden structure. When the sirens went off and the red flags came out, Marie's family took the steps down there. They lived near the dockyards so many of the bombs were aimed at British and American ships. The Italian and German planes dropped mines as well; the mines floated down on thick green parachutes that disintegrated as soon as they hit the water, and then the mines floated in the shipping lanes.

As my mother describes it, the boathouse had a big open space as soon as you entered, with lots of shelves on the walls to hold canoes and small boats. There would normally be ten or twelve people in there during the raids. They'd sit on wooden benches where they'd wait, they'd listen, and they'd pray. Praying bound them together—the English (mostly Protestant) and the Maltese (mostly Catholic). They prayed for each other and even for the English couple in their house hunkering down by themselves in the stairwell.

One night the sirens started wailing and Marie's family made a mad dash down the stairs to the boathouse, already having fallen asleep in their siren suits. It was an especially violent raid, and at one point the English couple suddenly burst into the boathouse among the dozen or so people. They dropped to their knees and started repeating, "Please God, save us! Please God, save us!" In those days most people called on God to keep them safe.

Later that night an enormous blast knocked everyone to the ground in the shelter. They all huddled on the floor together as the planes finished dropping their bombs and droned off into the night. Once the all-clear siren sounded, my mother's family and the couple stumbled outside to find their homes had taken a direct hit.

THERE WAS A LOT OF PRAYING GOING ON IN THAT BOATHOUSE—NOT MUCH ELSE TO DO WITH BOMBS DROPPING OUT OF THE SKY.

My mother doesn't know what happened to the English couple after that night—if they continued to pray or went back to their old ways in another stairwell; since their homes were destroyed, they all had to find other places to live. But at least for one night on Malta—and probably the rest of the war—prayer guided both believers and nonbelievers to safety.

People quickly rallied around my mother's family—Protestants and Catholics, English and Maltese. Under those circumstances people of all different religions and nationalities helped one another. Marie's family first stayed with a Maltese man who invited them to his hotel, then with a baroness that Marie's mother knew who opened up a ballroom in her mansion that they shared with another family. Another Maltese family offered them shelter during the air raids in a room that was all boarded up in their home. Marie and her family got buried there during another bombing and had to be dug out of the rubble. Throughout that whole time they continued to pray. Speaking of those days, my mother would tell me, "God doesn't look around and think, *She hasn't spoken to me in years, why is she asking for help now?* It's simply what you do during times like those. You ask for help, and it's a very good thing and you hope God is listening. There is no time limit on praying—anywhere, anytime, silently or loudly, sometimes or always. God is like a good friend or neighbor who you can call on at any time and he is always at home."

My mother, uncle, and grandmother left Malta before the end of the war, when Marie was fourteen. Like many other people, they were starving. They got passage on a bomber going to Cairo, Egypt, allowed to take exactly twenty-two pounds of baggage between the three of them. They had no seats—they sat on the floor. The whole experience made my mother braver than she might normally have been—stronger willed, with a more resilient character. But not bitter or hateful. Like those who have lived through dark times, she learned about the strength of the human spirit and acquired a great respect for the power and love of community.

In difficult times—individually or among nations—prayer brings people together. It may be a solitary act, but when we pray we are never alone. Prayer is a very private action but always binds us to a community. It teaches us humility and that it is okay to ask help from God and from the people around us. Hopefully at some point the English couple realized their first step on the path to salvation that night was not dropping to their knees and begging God for help but simply joining the small and devout community in that little boathouse.

8.

I WILL GIVE

I surf on a consistent basis at one of the most crowded surf spots in the world: Rincon, in Southern California. Rincon is known as the "Queen of the Coast"—arguably the best single wave in the entire state of California. Its long and beautiful waves give surfers fast, exciting rides. In fall and winter, swells wrap around a point of land and break all the way down toward Highway 101. When Rincon is firing, everyone within a hundred miles wants to catch a wave there. One morning during a new swell I hit the beach just as the sun was coming up. I jumped into the water down by the Cove, started my paddle up to the point, and began counting heads.

I stopped when I reached two hundred.

Two hundred surfers out at Rincon. Dealing with crowds isn't just a problem in surfing. Sports are getting more popular everywhere, and ultimately it's a good thing for all of us to stay active and enjoy ourselves. No matter what activity you like to

I still love to surf at Rincon and still try to push myself. A long time ago I put the bad experience I had there behind me. Photograph by Glenn Dubock.

do, we all have to learn how to deal with people in public spaces in a way that's not going to make us feel frustrated and ruin the very thing we like to do. On crowded days in the surf, guys get angry and yell at other surfers; sometimes there are fights. I know from personal experience about violence in the water. I learned one of the most important lessons of my life by getting punched in the face.

▲▼▲▼▲▼▲▼▲▼▲

The incident happened in the early '80s at Rincon. A big winter swell had rolled through: eight to ten feet on the bigger sets— a fantastic swell at a break that really suits my style of broad carves on long walls of water. I remember paddling out and seeing this one guy fly by me on a wave. I said to myself, *All right, this guy's a good surfer.* In those days there weren't a lot of really good surfers at Rincon. The place had dropped into a time warp of sorts. Many guys rode longboards, which at the time wasn't the popular style. Surfers wore black wetsuits and remained pretty conservative. This was in part a reaction against the neon lifestyle that'd taken hold a few hours to the south in Orange County at places like Newport Beach. My point is there were guys at Rincon who felt like they needed to protect the wave from outsiders.

The water was very cold that day. Oftentimes when the swell is big at Rincon you have to wait a long time for the sets to come through. The swells are born from storms in the Aleutian Islands, off the coast of Alaska, and travel thousands of miles before landing on the shores of Southern California, so you have to be patient. I'd been waiting quite a while for a wave—long enough to start shivering and for that good surfer I'd seen earlier to finish his ride and paddle right up next to me. Sure enough, a wave popped up on the horizon.

I swung around and paddled for it. The guy had seen the wave too and was moving with me. What he did was paddle around the back of me to get the inside position. In simple terms he jumped the line. We both caught the wave. I saw him drop down behind me, and I made my bottom turn right in front of him—basically blocked the guy out of the wave. Why did I do this? Because it was my turn. I'd waited, and he'd taken the wave on the previous set. So I took this one. It was a late takeoff for both of us on a big wave, and I assume he had a wipeout. I rode all the way down to the Cove, a good ride. I kept surfing for another few hours. I'd recently come back from spending the entire winter in Hawai'i, so I was in great shape and quite used to surfing big waves. I had a tremendous session that day.

So I dropped in on the surfer who'd paddled around me, spent several memorable hours in the water at a world-class surf spot, and that's the first part of my story. The second part is where I get punched.

Later that afternoon I'm hanging out at the beach with a girl I was dating. We're sitting on a low wall that overlooks the surf, just relaxing and chatting. Every once in a while a big set would roll through, and we'd check out the waves and the surfers carving long turns on the glassy faces.

This guy walks up to me. "Hey," he says, "aren't you Shaun Tomson?"

Now most of the time when people come up to me on the beach, it's a positive experience. They just want to meet and talk story, maybe introduce me to their kids. Sometimes if they're young they ask for an autograph. It always makes me feel good. There are a lot of good vibes in surfing, and one of the best things about the sport is that the youngest beginning surfer can sit in the water and share waves with the best surfer in the world. The only dividing lines in the sport are those created by Mother Nature. So I'm sitting with my girlfriend feeling really stoked about the day. I'm thinking, *All right, man. This guy wants to talk surf.*

Obviously I don't recognize him. He's not wearing his wet-suit, and he's got two buddies with him. I guess I wasn't really paying attention.

He says, "You dropped in on me."

Maybe it's the tone of his voice that tips me off, but all of a sudden I realize what's happening. He's standing there with his fists clenched and his friends on either side of him—all very aggressive. I'd gotten punched several years before by members of a Hawaiian gang on the North Shore for what they perceived as disrespect to them. My life was threatened at the time, and at one point I bought a Remington twelve-gauge shotgun because I had every intention of protecting myself if it came down to that. It never did, thankfully, but I'd experienced much worse situations, so I stand my ground with this guy.

"I waited for that wave," I tell him. "You paddled straight around on my inside. So yeah, I dropped in on you."

He starts yelling at me and cussing me out. I'm not interested in dealing with this guy at all. I remember turning away and pretty much dismissing him. My girlfriend is sitting to my left. As I turn my head to say something to her—*Boom!*—the guy punches me right on the side of the face.

I'm totally taken by surprise. Later on I find out this guy has hassled other surfers and been involved in a number of brawls on the beach. I jump off the wall onto the sand. He starts throwing kicks at my head, martial-arts style, and his friends move in from either side.

A small digression: the heavy cobblestones lining Rincon Point are the main reason why the wave breaks so well and so consistently. Beach-break waves peel off underwater sandbars, which are always shifting around from storm to storm and season to season. But the cobblestones at Rincon are more or less permanent, and so the waves break in a very predictable pattern. This is great for practicing surf maneuvers. It's also convenient if you happen to need something heavy to throw.

I'm doing my best to block his kicks, and before the thing turns into an absolute brawl, I grab one of the cobblestones and say, "Any of you guys come near me, and you're going to get a rock on the head."

WE ALL HAVE TO LEARN HOW TO DEAL WITH PEOPLE IN PUBLIC SPACES IN A WAY THAT'S NOT GOING TO MAKE US FEEL FRUSTRATED AND RUIN THE VERY THING WE LIKE TO DO.

Fortunately I don't have to heave cobblestones at anybody, and the situation diffuses—with a bit more yelling and cussing for good measure.

Afterward I go to the police and file charges. Both my girlfriend and I give statements. Ultimately the district attorney prosecutes the guy for felony assault. It was one of the first times a surfer complained to the police about behavior that was more or less accepted in the surf community. Maybe the DA acted on the complaint because I was a fairly high-profile person in surfing.

I think now that my complaint to the police was an important first step to changing people's attitudes about what's acceptable behavior in the surf. But at the time I didn't really care that they arrested him, or even later on convicted him. I wanted to forget about the whole experience. I surfed Rincon again, but not with the same enthusiasm. To have that sort of violence happen after a surf session really left a sour taste in my mouth. And for months afterward I had the worst feeling in and out of the water just knowing that a guy could lose control like that and actually punch someone over a single wave. I left Santa Barbara not too long afterward to rejoin the World Tour, and I didn't come back to Rincon for a number of years, even though I loved the wave.

The guy was clearly in the wrong. He hadn't waited his turn in the lineup. He'd paddled around me to get into the wave. And he'd overreacted when he saw me on the beach. And our meeting was no accident: he'd seen me and waited for the best time to confront me.

But what would've happened if I'd given him that wave?

I would've waited—perhaps a few seconds, even a few minutes—for another wave in the set. I would've taken that wave into shore and probably gotten a great ride. And I would've paddled back out and stroked into more great waves. I would not have gotten punched in front of my girlfriend and been

Off the Wall, North Shore, Hawai'i, 1977. One of the best waves of my life behind
Mark Richards, who went on to win four world titles and revolutionize surfing with
his twin fin design. Photograph by Lance Trout.

part of an ugly scene on the beach. And most importantly I would've returned to Rincon more often—wouldn't have had those terrible memories of the place—and enjoyed surfing its magical waves.

It's hard to see people get things they don't deserve. To let a wave go by, for instance, or to step back if someone is being too aggressive. No one likes to give ground or be taken advantage of. Especially in a crowded situation when other people might be looking on. How do you know when to give?

Here's what I tell myself before I paddle out in crowded conditions: *There will always be another wave; there will always be another surf session.* If I prepare myself in advance for what might happen—people taking too many waves or dropping in front of me—I go a long way to ensuring that rude or aggressive behavior doesn't ruin an experience that I want to be positive. Knowing that I have the confidence to give in those situations— to keep my cool and realize I'll be back to surf another day— ensures that I'll enjoy those beautiful waves every time they roll into Rincon.

9.

I WILL MAKE A DIFFERENCE

When I was a teenager, a young black African named Ernest Bongani Nkosi came to work for my family in Durban. A relative of one of our housekeepers, Ernest was a few years younger than I was, and we became friends. At the time, South Africa was a segregated society under the political system called apartheid: blacks, whites, Indians, and coloureds (people of mixed race) moved in separate spheres and were discouraged from mingling with one another. This system began after the election of the National Party in 1948 and finally ended with the election of Nelson Mandela—a black African—as president in 1994.

Apartheid, as the name implies, was a system developed to keep the various races apart in South Africa, and each race lived in its own area defined by a group of laws called the Group Areas Act. Blacks were forcibly removed from their land into separate townships, providing reservoirs of cheap labor for the white population. We had something like 85 percent of the black population living on 15 percent of the land, a recipe for poverty and social decay.

Ernest grew up as one of five children in a poor, single-parent household and so had to start working as a gardener on Saturdays for white people. He was twelve at the time—rather young to understand all the political dynamics—and so he struggled a lot with the hostile attitudes and treatment that he experienced outside his township. Basically we lived in a racist society, and white people treated Ernest as a second-class citizen. When he came to work for my family, he experienced what he called "humane treatment," although for us it was simply our normal way of interacting with people. When the famous Hawaiian surfer Eddie Aikau came to South Africa to surf in the Gunston 500 in 1971 and had trouble at the whites-only hotel because of his dark skin, my father invited him to stay with us. This was basic courtesy for Eddie, and we extended the same to Ernest. He was bright and ambitious, a hard worker, and I encouraged him.

Later, when Ernest was fourteen he started working at my dad's surf shop in Durban. It was steadier work than the family garden, and he did odd jobs and learned how to repair surf-boards. He once mentioned a white guy who'd get mad at him for whatever reason and say, "Ernest, what the hell do you think you are?" The guy said "what," not "who," as if Ernest were not even a human being. Because Ernest was a young black man in that time and place, the question always paralyzed him. The white guy was basically telling Ernest, "Your future is hopeless, you'll never amount to anything." It was the kind of comment that unfortunately was all too common in South Africa. The guy was probably jealous of Ernest because of how close he was to our family. My brother, Paul—three years younger than I am—built up a strong friendship with Ernest in those years, and they often played together. It's amazing to think that in such a racially hostile society two young people could develop such trust and affection for one another. I've always felt that one of the real strengths of young people is that they have open hearts, and this inevitably leads to open minds.

Ernest was ambitious, as I've said, and it was very discouraging for him to hear those comments; they contributed to a terrible image he had of himself. But the support he felt from my family gave him the courage one day to stand up to this guy. Ernest finally told him, "It is not about what I think I am, but the knowledge that I am somebody, created out of God's image." The white guy walked away after that and never troubled him again. That moment gave Ernest an enormous boost of confidence, and he told me that he doubted he would have been able to imagine doing something like that for himself if not for the encouragement from me and my family.

In the late '70s and early '80s I traveled the world most of the year surfing on the professional tour. I was back in South Africa for the Gunston 500 when I ran into Ernest on the beach. By then my dad had passed away and the rest of my family had moved to the United States. Ernest and I had dinner together, and I asked him how he was doing. He'd been accepted at Umbumbulu College of Education, a three-year program for teachers, but it turned out he couldn't afford to go because of the tuition. To me that was unacceptable, and I offered to help pay his way through school. It was a simple enough gesture on my part, and I didn't think much about it. He was a friend, and I wanted to make a difference in his life, however small. We lost touch in the 1990s after I became an American citizen and moved to the United States.

꘏꘏꘏꘏꘏

In 2011 Ernest got in touch with me again. I was giving a talk in Johannesburg, which is the largest city in South Africa and about 350 miles inland from where I grew up in Durban. He said that he'd come to Mathew's funeral back in 2006, but I honestly don't remember seeing him. That whole time was so painful for me and Carla, I really don't remember seeing anyone.

SOMETIMES A SINGLE GESTURE OF GOODWILL, AN ENCOURAGING WORD, CAN MAKE ALL THE DIFFERENCE IN A PERSON'S LIFE.

But I wanted to reconnect with Ernest and so I had him flown to Johannesburg so that he could attend my talk. It was a big charity event to support Cotlands—a nonprofit group that helps children—and I Care—an organization that works to rehabilitate street kids in South Africa and reintegrate them into society. My talk was called "The Light Shines Ahead," inspired by the events surrounding Mathew's death. I learned that Ernest had become the principal of Qhilika High School in Durban and was responsible for the education and well-being of 1,600 young South Africans. He'd managed to earn two university degrees and two teaching credentials under the oppressive system of apartheid. I singled him out during my talk and said that I was proud of him. Ernest was originally going to use his college degree as a stepping-stone in life until he started teaching and came into contact with the hard realities of young people in Umlazi. Most of the kids are either raised by grand-parents or raise themselves in what are called "child-headed" families. Students often come to school with empty stomachs and worn-out pants, shirts, and shoes. There are great celebra-tions every year at Qhilika High School for the students who graduate despite harsh poverty. There is also great sadness for those who don't make it through because of drugs, pregnancy, crime, and suicide. Ernest and his students fight the realities of overcrowded classrooms and lack of resources every day. I told the crowd that Ernest was a shining example for those students; a man who didn't accept the limitations imposed on him, but rather used those limitations to motivate himself to be a better human being. Ernest is now making a difference in the lives of thousands of young people who have the chance to transcend their past and transform South Africa.

After the talk Ernest asked me if I would come visit his school to speak with some of the students and give them the same encouragement that I had given him so many years ago.

⋀⋀⋀⋀⋀⋀

Qhilika is located in a very impoverished area of Durban. There is no auditorium at the school, so I spoke to the kids in a church. They were all well dressed in their uniforms: blue slacks and ties for the boys, blue skirts for the girls, and all of them in neatly pressed blazers. They were very attentive. Ernest spoke before I did. He introduced me and told the students about his life grow-ing up in Durban and the difference that my family and I had made for him. Many of the township kids don't know that there

HAWKS PROBE FRAUD. CORRUPTION CHARGES

Shaun Tomson goes head to head with long-time friend Bongani Nkosi, principal of Umlazi's Qhilika High School. PICTURE: DOCTOR NGCOBO

Baldwin Ndaba
and Omphitlhetse Mooki

SUSPENDED crime intelligence head Richard Mdluli handed himself over to the Hawks yesterday following fresh allegations of fraud and corruption against him.

Mdluli, a lieutenant-general in the SAPS, was suspended earlier this year after being charged with murder, a count unrelated to his current problem.

The Mercury's sister newspaper The Star understands that Mdluli handed himself over to the Hawks following the unit's consolidation of misappropriation of witness protection funds and false police claims charges against him.

Police investigators have reportedly discovered information that Mdluli allegedly used money from the fund to pay salaries and to buy houses and cars for girlfriends and their relatives as well as his own relatives, who had been registered as covert intelligence operatives.

In one case, investigators found that a Cape Town woman, who they reportedly confirmed as his girlfriend, was registered as an intelligence operative and was paid at least R18 000 a month. The girlfriend's cousin and brother were also allegedly "employed" by crime intelligence and earned R8 000 a month.

"She lives in a house and drives a BMW bought by SAPS funds. These people were paid and lived off the state for doing nothing," a source said.

It is understood that investigators

Surfing star Tomson renews brotherly bond

Suren Naidoo

A BROTHERLY bond was renewed yesterday when Durban-born surfing star and businessman Shaun Tomson met up again with longtime friend Bongani Nkosi.

Tomson gave a riveting talk to 200 Grade 10 youngsters at Umlazi's Qhilika High School at the invitation of Nkosi.

The two struck up a friendship in the 1970s that ultimately saw Tomson sponsor Nkosi's education. Yesterday Nkosi got Tomson

to go to Umlazi to "motivate and inspire" his pupils with his incredible life story and lessons.

Tomson lives in California and Nkosi had not seen him since 2006, when Tomson's teenage son Matthew died in an accident.

"I found out Shaun was coming to South Africa to speak at a conference in Joburg. I... contacted him to tell him how grateful I was for what he had done for me. I also told him I was the principal of a school in Umlazi and really wanted him to come to speak to the kids," said Nkosi.

"Seeing Shaun here taking time out to speak to our pupils is really great... It takes me back to my childhood, when he used to always encourage me. Today, he inspired the youngsters to work hard, persevere and that they can make it despite their situation, just like I have," he said.

Tomson said Nkosi was an inspiration in himself and he was proud of his achievements.

"I just gave Bongani a push and a little helping hand in life. He did it all on his own to get where he is today... He has got two teaching

degrees and is the principal of a school. It could not be better because he is a leader giving back now in a selfless job. He's an incredible guy and has devoted his life to making our country better through its children – our future," he said.

"It was a wonderful experience talking to the youngsters. They have a great spirit and enthusiasm... The group I spoke to were all born post-1994. They need to look to the future, get a good education and make South Africa great," added Tomson.

Reuniting with Ernest Bongani Nkosi, a truly inspirational teacher and leader in South Africa. From *The Mercury*.

were friendly relations between different races during apartheid, and it was important for Ernest to tell them these stories for the reconciliation and nation-building that is necessary for South Africa's future. Apartheid may have ended in the 1990s but the deep wounds of racial oppression and segregation take a long time to heal. Ernest is a gifted speaker, very emotional and empowering. He was dignified and firm but very empathetic—a born leader. He stressed the power of hard work and discipline to them. He said, "Don't blame other people or apartheid for your problems." Ernest had proven to them with the story of his life that it is possible to succeed if you are resolute and committed. And because he had been encouraged on his steep and winding path through apartheid, he encouraged them as well. He believes that everyone who encourages and helps others is also encouraged and helped.

I join with Ernest in believing that with the right attitude and commitment anything is possible for the current generation. Ernest quoted Genesis to them: "While the earth remains, seedtime and harvest, cold and heat, summer and winter, day and night, shall not cease." It's his way of telling them not to be tempted by shortcuts; their goals can be achieved if they move away from the child's desire for easy answers and accept the responsibility that comes with being an adult.

Ernest was a tough act to follow. I was so honored to be there—in his presence, at his school—and to see the impact that he was making on those kids. It made me feel like I'd done something important.

After I spoke, two of the students addressed the group with poise and dignity. From their example I could tell Ernest had made a profound impact on their lives. Though raised in poverty, they were not poor in spirit or intelligence. They were the faces of the new South Africa, of the country's future, and I couldn't help but think of Ernest's words: *Those who encourage and help others are also encouraged and helped.* Ernest had asked me to come and encourage these students, and I sat in that church with my spirits soaring, so inspired by how much Ernest and his students were achieving together. Helping another person can be such a simple act, and we never know where it will lead or how many lives will be affected. Sometimes a single gesture of goodwill, an encouraging word, can make all the difference in a person's life, or even in the life of a nation.

Students at the high school work with the Olive Leaf Foundation, helping other impoverished kids in the area by starting a sustainable food garden. In 2009 the Qhilika Kidz Club began harvesting vegetables from their garden to give to local orphanages. The Olive Leaf Foundation writes: "One of the results of this enterprise is that the youths feel empowered to do more in their community as they recognize their potential to make a positive impact on the lives of others." They started with one garden, and soon had four up and running. The goodwill keeps growing in Umlazi. Ernest himself started working as a gardener outside his township all those years ago. Though a principal now, he remains dedicated to the ideals of seedtime and harvest, of putting the work in every day so that his students see the impact he is making in their lives and that they are making in the new and vibrant life of South Africa.

10.

I WILL IMAGINE

There are some days when I don't even see the beach, let alone paddle out for a session. I have my business, my responsibilities, and so it's important for me to find a way to bring the beach into my life, if only for a few moments. Surfers call this *mind surfing*. You can mind surf a wave as you stand on the edge of a cliff and watch a swell march into your local beach, or you can mind surf a wave sitting behind a desk at work or school. If you've surfed long enough, mind surfing kicks in automatically when your brain starts to combust from the stress of daily life. It's like air conditioning for the spirit, only more refreshing. Here's the best part: mind surfing isn't an escape from my everyday work; it helps me work better.

I need surfing now more than ever before. Once in a while I need a break from the stress and complexities of life. I'll be at work and tell myself, *Man, it'd be just great to paddle out and get one good wave.* I close my eyes and the frames start clicking away.

When the conditions were right, the Bay of Plenty offered up a challenging and exciting tube ride. Photograph by Jeff Divine.

I'm back home in Durban, South Africa. I feel the cold sand under my feet and a stiff offshore blowing at my back. But the sand and wind are not what's giving me goose bumps. It's 1974, and I'm staring at a new swell pounding the Bay of Plenty, my home beach.

I lean down on one knee and start rubbing wax over the deck of my board, making steady circular motions from tail to nose. My heart pounds with every wave that detonates off the sand bar, and I know that I'm either going to get the ride of my life today or I'm going to wash up the beach with a broken back. I stop waxing and look up and down the beach. No one's around.

So I have a decision to make. How badly do I really want it?

Just those few moments give me a wonderful, vicarious feeling. My blood is pumping again. I click back to reality: I'm refreshed and ready to tackle life again.

All surfers have one special wave they recall vividly. Go ahead and ask sometime. You'll get an instant smile, a shake of the head like they still can't believe that it happened. They'll begin to describe random details—how cold the water felt that day, the color of the sky, the sensation of wind on their face as they dropped wide eyed into that one miracle wave. And because words are not enough to convey the full experience (are they ever?), surfers begin to move their hands and bend their bodies this way and that as if to conjure that wave and that moment back to life. If you saw them from a distance, you just might think they were casting a spell. A surfer will be standing in front of you and talking, but his eyes or her voice will tell you they're locked in a wave miles, perhaps continents, away.

I've had many great surf sessions. I've been fortunate to ride swells at Jeffreys Bay, at the tip of South Africa, that lasted so long my legs gave out. I've surfed Pipeline, on the North Shore of O'ahu, at its very best, and Sunset Beach, also on the North Shore, at its most dangerous. But the single greatest wave of my life occurred that day in 1974 in Durban. I say greatest not so much because of its size or shape, though certainly both were memorable, but in the particular way this wave tested my imagination.

⋀⋁⋀⋁⋀⋁⋀⋁⋀

A good south swell has hit the Bay of Plenty, which is the best swell for the bay. It's a real gloomy day late in the afternoon, dead low tide. We'd get very low tides at certain times of the year in Durban. Storm systems from Antarctica pounded the beaches in the wintertime and created a ferocious riptide that ran along the beach and dumped truckloads of sand at the end of a jetty, where it formed a tremendously long sand point. There's not much resistance from the continental shelf in this part of Africa, so the waves roll in very fast and very strong. On this particular day the swell is so big, and the waves sucking so strongly off the bottom, that if I manage to catch a wave out there, I'll actually be riding *below* that sandbar.

I brought a longer board than usual to the beach, a 7'7" that I normally only rode in the Hawaiian Islands on a big day. As I sit on the sand and watch wave after wave pound the shore, I'm thinking, *This swell can't be surfed.* The waves are simply coming in too fast and breaking in too shallow of water. But every so often a wave hits the sandbar and peels perfectly. A freight train, certainly, but one I might manage to hang onto with the longer board. If I commit to the wrong wave, I'll get driven headfirst into that sandbar. But if I pick the right wave ...

HOW THIN THAT LINE IS BETWEEN DOUBT AND IMAGINATION, BETWEEN SUCCESS AND FAILURE.

I jump into the riptide, knowing there's only one way back to the beach. As soon as the rip pulls me beyond the jetty, I start to prowl the impact zone: I paddle for a wave, then back off. I paddle for another, back off again. It's very frustrating. I've got so much adrenaline pumping through my body; I want to catch a wave, but I have to consider the possibility that I was right after all, and the swell simply can't be surfed.

As I sit and mull this over, rising and falling with these enormous swells surging underneath me, it occurs to me for the first time that I won't be able to tell which wave is going to hold up until I've already dropped down the face.

To hell with it, I say finally, and I paddle into a big one.

At this extreme low tide, a lot of sand is sucking up the wave face. As I make my bottom turn and look down the line, I think, *You've just made the biggest mistake of your life.* The wave looks like a sand cavern. Only it's moving—fast—and now closing down on top of me. If I'd bailed out right then—tried to use the momentum from my drop to punch my board through the back of the wave—I might've made it.

I'll never know.

I have one line on that wave, and one line only, and I hold onto it, my feet pressing into the wax. It grows very dark inside, and this is where I lose track of what happens exactly when. I see an eye of light at the end flashing open and closed, now giving me hope, now shutting it down. I remember focusing on that tiny portal as it telescopes farther and farther away from me. I'm falling, at that point, farther and farther back from the light, getting sucked back into the tunnel, and I think, *You're not going to make it now—you're too far back.*

I'm in a very dangerous position: racing low on the wall right over the sandbar. If my board was any lower, my outside rail would catch and I would instantly get slammed into the hard-packed sand. The section of wave ahead is mindless: walled up as far as I can see. No chance of escape at all.

In these extreme situations there's always the tendency to jump. Just bail off the back of the board and throw your arms in front of your face. Take the hit you know is coming. And sooner rather than later, because more speed is only going to make things worse. At least you've chosen the moment, right?

It's fear that tears us down, and lack of imagination: *I can't keep this pace. I can't ride any deeper. It's not possible to go any faster on a surfboard and survive.*

If I'd had the slightest cushion of water beneath me, I might've jumped.

Suddenly I hear the wave explode behind me. All this foam flies past—I feel it drive into my body like a gale—and it blows with such force that it actually lifts the board right off the water, and me with it.

My board and I are flying along completely out of the water now, inside the barrel, carried along by this blast of supercompressed air. I'm twenty or thirty feet back in the tube, with this amazing sensation of flying through the air on a surfboard. Suddenly the board drops back down onto the surface of the water, and I come bursting out of the barrel into daylight.

No spectators are screaming on the beach; no voices droning point totals over the PA system or camera shutters clicking away. I hear only the sound of the wind. And as I drift over the shoulder, I look back down to where I might've been—out in the white water tumbling around had I jumped off my board. How thin that line is between doubt and imagination, between success and failure.

Every surfer has a similar story. One moment they're being dragged into oblivion, the next they're flying along on the very breath of the wave. The feeling of time being expanded and distorted, of fear and exhilaration all melded together—these are rare sensations that replenish the spirit and sustain the soul.

A well-known poem by William Butler Yeats hangs above my desk at work, and I look at it every day: "An Irish Airman Foresees His Death." The last four lines have always reminded me of that wave in the Bay of Plenty:

I balanced all, brought all to mind,
The years to come seemed waste of breath,
A waste of breath the years behind
In balance with this life, this death.

I have so many associations when I read these lines: the sensation of flight, like the airman in the poem; the breath of the wave; the sense of danger; the commitment to fly in the face of that danger; and the importance of balance and imagination. But over all of these is the ultimate decision to live in the moment and to choose one path and follow wherever it takes me. That path is not a destination (which no surfer is ever concerned with while on a wave) but simply living with passion. And I gain an enormous sense of calm knowing that I chose a path not for prize money or the praise of others, but for what Yeats terms "A lonely impulse of delight." In the end I followed my passion.

I see a complementary relationship between our actions in life and our imaginations: each defines, and is defined by, the other. And this holds true for my surfing. The more I surf, the more possibilities open up to me; and the more possibilities I can imagine, the better my surfing becomes. And the richer the entire surfing experience.

And because surfing stays with me after I leave the waves—in the salt on my skin, the pleasant ache in my shoulders, that general sense of well-being that warms my whole body like a summer day—I can draw on those physical sensations to nourish the imagination and invigorate my life every day.

11.

I WILL HAVE FAITH

Life was great for the Tomson family in 2006. Carla and I had recently sold our apparel business, Solitude—which we'd started back in 1998—to Oxford Industries, a billion-dollar company traded on the New York Stock Exchange. They'd funded a stylish new design studio for us near our home in Montecito and put us on a three-year contract. We had a great relationship with both the CEO and president, and they were eager to expand the brand. We couldn't have been more excited about the future.

Our son Mathew was fifteen at the time and having some problems academically at the local high school. We decided that a semester at Clifton, my old private school in South Africa, would be a great way for him to get his grades up and reconnect with our homeland. The plan was for Carla to go there with him. I'd join them before he finished out the semester, and we'd all return home together.

I drove them to the Santa Barbara Airport in late January. We said our goodbyes, and I watched as they stood in line to go through security. Mathew was tall and handsome. I saw him then with new eyes, one of those moments as a parent when you realize that your child is no longer a child. He was a young man with his whole life ahead of him. I was proud to be his father. He'd slung a small backpack over his shoulder. It made him look vulnerable for some reason: a schoolboy in a man's skin, embarking on a long journey, his mom at his side. I felt a terrible wave of regret and foreboding—the familiar dread that rises up at times of separation: *Stop the trip! Don't let them go!* But the moment passed quickly, and I did nothing. They disappeared through the security gate into the departure lounge.

Within a month Mathew was doing great, excelling at my old school. He wore a uniform every day—long pants, a blazer, and tie—and he was thriving in the structured post-apartheid environment.

At 9 a.m. on April 24, Carla and I had a three-way business call scheduled with the New York office. I called South Africa from home. Mathew picked up right away. It felt like he was sitting next to me. He was happy and excited, told me he was playing his first rugby game the next day.

"Hey, Dada," he said. "I want to read you something."

Curious, I pulled the phone closer.

"Deep inside the barrel," he began, "completely in tune with my inner self, nothing else matters, the hard wind and spit shooting past me from behind, my hand dragging along the wall, the light shines ahead."

I listened as he read for a minute or so. When he finished, I asked him who wrote those beautiful words.

"I did, Dada." Pride filled his voice. Four of the words—*the light shines ahead*—stayed with me afterward, cycling through my mind like a favorite song. Mathew had captured the essence of the surfing experience with a simplicity and depth of spirituality rare for a fifteen-year-old.

Carla jumped on the line. We had to start the conference call.

"I love you, Dada."

"I love you too, Mathew."

I'd see him in two weeks. I'd already sent away my passport for new pages. Mathew knew I was coming, and we were going to surprise Carla.

At 10 a.m. a photographer and journalist from a Japanese surf magazine picked me up at the design studio. They'd flown in for an interview and wanted to take some pictures to fill out the story. Of course I took them to Hammond's Reef, my local break and the site of the sacred story circle that I talk more about in the next chapter.

It was a magnificent spring day, warm and bright. We walked down the short trail—a picturesque spot for their article—winding through a grove of tall eucalyptus trees. The trail ends at a small wooden bridge where you get a first glimpse at the ocean. I looked out at the Pacific, shimmering blue in the morning light. It was beautiful, sharply focused, a postcard shot of the perfect beach, the perfect life in Montecito, California.

Back on the path I had a profound feeling of unease. I stopped under a large eucalyptus tree. The interviewer stopped with me.

"Nothing is more important than a positive attitude," I said. We'd been chatting for some time. I believed what I said, but the statement sounded forced for some reason, overconfident, as if I had the knowledge of life in the palm of my hand, dispensing my worldly wisdom to his readers.

We got in the car for the drive back to the studio. My cell phone rang.

It was Carla. I heard only three words: "Mathew is dead."

Time stopped. Dead? I must have misheard. How was that possible? I'd just spoken with him. It was like watching someone else's life disintegrate before your eyes, someone else experiencing unbearable pain. I couldn't process the information. This couldn't be happening. How could I live without my son?

Now a friend's voice came on the other end. I understood only fragments. My beautiful son ... playing a risky game ... deadly consequences.

My life—our lives—destroyed in a moment.

/\/\/\/\/\/\/\

My friends in Santa Barbara rallied. They got me a passport, a ticket, and put me on a plane to South Africa.

It was a harrowing trip, a blur I barely remember. Except for two thoughts: saying a last goodbye to my boy, and holding Carla.

My beautiful son was gone. He died playing what is known as the choking game. Carla found him. She was devastated. When I arrived she had to be admitted to the hospital. I didn't think she was going to make it. She'd lost the will to live, and my focus shifted to saving her. I'd lost my son. I couldn't lose my wife and survive.

We stayed in the hospital together. We tried to deal with our terrible grief and pain. A psychiatrist visited every morning. "Time is your friend," he'd tell us. There was no escape from the enormity of the loss, the knowledge that we'd never hug our boy again. The pain was constant and unrelenting, from the time we woke up until we went to sleep. It even invaded our dreams. Both of us were lost. Carla's mom, Vivienne, flew in from London. My sister, Tracy, arrived from San Diego. We might not have recovered without their help. Our remaining family and friends in South Africa rushed to our aid; still we spiraled into depression, those depths where it's easy to lose faith—to close your eyes and block out the nightmare.

After two weeks in the hospital, a close friend came to visit. He stood at the foot of Carla's bed in the small room. He too had lost a son, had been on this same terrible journey. Carla and I were aware that he had sought comfort through meditation and from a grief counselor that he believed was connected to the afterlife.

Without preamble he said, "I have a message from Mathew."

As he said those words a single bolt of lightning hit the hospital, followed by an enormous clap of thunder. I looked out the window on a clear, cloudless sky. I looked at Carla, at her mom sitting on the bed next to her. Had they seen that? Had they heard what I just heard?

"He said he made a mistake and wants you to forgive him. What he did was an accident."

That moment marked a turning point in our recovery and our slow journey back to life. Had our friend made Mathew's death easier to accept? No. But he gave us a connection to life beyond earth. And to Mathew. Knowing that Mathew was still present in spirit gave us the faith to move forward.

⁘⁘⁘⁘⁘⁘

It's been a long and difficult road to recovery. Losing a child goes against the natural order, an enormous void so difficult to fill. I've discovered it is futile and self-destructive to live in the world of conjecture, in the world of *what if* rather than *what is*. The world of *what if* would have destroyed Carla and me.

The community shared in our pain and gave of themselves. Friends cooked dinners, doctors refused payment, supporters

When we lost Mathew we never thought we'd be a happy family again, but Luke came along and changed our lives. Photographs from the Tomson Collection.

sent messages from around the world. Everyone wanted to share their love and give us help. Without that love we might never have recovered.

As with the death of my father, I dreaded going surfing again. Then about a month after Mathew died a friend took me to a break I'd never surfed before. Just the two of us in the water on a beautiful day. I paddled out, and I cried and cried. I finally took a wave, and that ride started my path to healing.

I asked my friend, "What's this break called?"

"Sunrise," he said.

I thought of the last words Mathew had read to me over the phone—*the light shines ahead*—and I smiled because I knew he was close.

A married couple heals differently after the loss of a child. We received help from doctors, rabbis, our family and friends. We learned there's no one way to grieve. Carla dealt with our loss through introspection. I threw myself into new projects, all of which I dedicated to Mathew. His words of hope resonated deeply with me every day.

Each day the pain became less severe, and Carla and I grew closer. We were like two trees that had fallen in a storm. We'd toppled against one other, shored each other up, then grew together. Through all the damage we held out hope that we'd be a family again one day.

On August 25, 2009, we received an unexpected phone call from our lawyer. We'd tried adopting a baby once already, but the birth mother changed her mind at the last minute. It was an emotional roller coaster for us, and we weren't strong enough to endure that long process again.

When our lawyer told us that a baby boy had been born just before midnight the previous day and asked if we were interested in adopting, Carla and I immediately said yes.

But there were issues. Under California law, a birth mother may pick the parents for her child. This particular mother was already considering a number of families, and we were at the back of the line.

The baby had been born a month premature. Its original birth date was September 25, Mathew's birthday.

"This is a sign from God," Carla told me. "This is our baby."

We submitted a detailed profile on our family. The birth mother wanted a photo of Mathew. We got another call back from our lawyer telling us that she had planned to give the baby the same name: Mathew.

We knew the baby had to be ours!

The next morning she made her decision, and we had our baby. We drove to the hospital immediately in a state of delirious happiness, the light shining ahead. My hero growing up as a young boy was the Hawaiian Duke Kahanamoku, the embodiment of the aloha spirit. He was also born on August 24, so from a surfer's perspective the baby's birth date couldn't have been more auspicious. We arrived at the hospital and were told to go directly to the nursery before meeting the woman who would share the precious gift of her child.

We walked into the nursery and held our little boy for the first time. Our rush of emotion was the same as when our beautiful Mathew was born. I felt no difference in the love for the child in my arms—the embrace, the connection, the bond were all the same. When he looked up at me, I saw Mathew in his face. He was not Mathew, of course, but the turn of events that had brought him to us were too strong to deny that a larger power was at work.

The birth mother has thirty days to change her decision. She is under no obligation to do anything she doesn't feel is right. We went to her room and looked at her lying on the bed like an angel. She was our angel, come to share a gift from God. She had an uncanny resemblance to my wife—she could have been her twin sister. It quite took my breath away. Carla noticed it as well. We all hugged. We were surrounded by this incredible warmth and emotion and love. She asked if our baby was beautiful. We said he was, and we thanked her for her trust, for sharing with us her most precious gift. We hugged again and left.

IT IS FUTILE AND SELF-DESTRUCTIVE TO LIVE IN THE WORLD OF CONJECTURE, IN THE WORLD OF "WHAT IF" RATHER THAN "WHAT IS."

Carla and I were overjoyed on the ride home. During our short visit with the birth mother, she'd asked us the baby's name. She wanted him to carry the name that we'd chosen. "Luke," we told her. The name felt right to us. Later we looked up the meaning. Why weren't we surprised to discover that Luke translates to "light," "bringer of light," or "healer"?

And so today our faith remains strong because we are a family again: Carla, me, and our two boys, Mathew and Luke, one a gift from God and the other a bringer of light.

12.

I WILL SHARE STORIES

Stories have been at the heart of surf culture going all the way back to the oral traditions of the Hawaiians. Surfing isn't a sport where you shoot eighteen holes, write the numbers on a scorecard, then go back the very next day and play that exact course again. Once you've ridden those waves, they're gone. All that remains is a trace of salt on your skin, a feeling of contentment in your soul, and a story or two. Every person should spend at least one summer evening at Ala Moana Beach on the south side of O'ahu, relaxing on the grass after a surf or swim, watching the sun go down, feeling the trade winds cool your skin, and listening to the locals tell one another stories. Not epics, not big dramas, just everyday stories. The most extraordinary experiences surround surfing, and many of them have little to do with actually riding waves. Here's one that comes to mind when I think of the importance of storytelling. It's been

One of the best moments of life was sitting with Mathew here on Hammond's Beach inside his sacred story circle. Photograph by Heidi Blair.

seven years since Carla and I lost Mathew—he passed away in 2006—and I tell this story because it connects me to him and keeps his spirit alive.

ΙΛΙΛΙΛΙΛΙΛΙΛΙΛΙΛΙ

I used to give Mathew surf lessons when he was growing up. He was interested in surfing—not obsessed with it as I was at his age—but we certainly paddled out together as often as possible. The closest break to our home is Hammond's Reef, a beautiful little beach that's typically uncrowded because of its secluded location. We usually drove in and followed one of the paths bordered with ice plant to a bench that sits on a grassy knoll overlooking the point. Behind us rose the wooded Santa Ynez Mountains filled with trails for hikers and bikers; before us lay the beach itself covered with gray cobblestones that ranged in size from softballs to watermelons and larger. Great tangles of driftwood gathered at the high-tide line, cast ashore by winter storms. From the bench we'd spot swells rolling through and also the remains of campfires among the cobblestones that visitors had dragged into rough circles. Mathew and I had our particular stones along the path, underneath which we stashed our bars of surf wax in case the swell was up and we decided to paddle out. When the waves are quiet and the wind dies down, the whole atmosphere at Hammond's is calming; the rhythmic sound of the waves, and the sun glinting off the surface of the water so that the ocean resembles nothing less than a field of sparkling diamonds—*sparkle factor* is in fact the expression surfers use to describe this condition—remind me of why I chose to live and work in Santa Barbara.

Hammond's is a special place for me because I shared it with my son. And beyond a touch of serenity in an otherwise hectic world, Hammond's is also home to a Chumash Indian memorial. Much of the coastline in this area was peopled by the Chumash. They thrived here for thousands of years before California's Mission Period in the late 1700s; places like Hammond's and Rincon down the coast served them as protected bays where they could launch their canoes in safety, and they used the natural tar seepages in the region to seal their small oceangoing craft. One day when Mathew and I were walking along the beach at Hammond's just checking the surf—he was nine at the time—he suddenly said to me, "Let's go up and visit the memorial."

SURFiNG iS ALL ABOUT UNCERTAiNTy. THAT FEELiNG OF TAKiNG A RiSK, THAT LEAP OF FAiTH EVERy TiME I JUMP iNTO THE OCEAN.

The memorial sits in Shalawa Meadow, a small clearing just south of the grassy knoll and back from the beach a ways. No more than a few minutes walk. The cobblestones along the shore give way to scrub brush and large rocks that are havens for lizards; gopher holes dot the meadow here and there, and the monument stands right in the middle of the clearing. It's four or five feet high, rectangular in shape, covered with decorative tiles on the side that faces the Pacific. In between a couple dolphin figurines are the following words:

> *The sacredness of the land*
> *lies in the minds of its people.*
> *This land is dedicated to*
> *the spirit and memory of*
> *the ancestors and their*
> *children.*

Around the base visitors leave various rocks and shells, flowers, driftwood, all pulled from the beach and set in a semicircle so that the memorial has the feeling of a small shrine. With the mountains rising behind the meadow and the Pacific stretching out as far as one can see, the area has that dramatic quietude common to ancient and spiritual places. One cannot help but think of all those who lived and enjoyed this terrain over the centuries—families, fishermen, entire communities—and all the people in centuries to come who will enjoy this meadow and the Pacific vista, and pay their respects to the land.

After Mathew and I had spent a few minutes gazing at the memorial and adding our own offerings, we walked back to the beach and suddenly he said to me, "Dada"—this is what he called me when his friends weren't around—"help me do this."

He started to pick up cobblestones, one at a time, and arrange them in a large circular shape right on the sand. "What is that you're making?" I asked him. He didn't answer, just kept adding stones to complete the circle. I started to help him without knowing why, simply because he'd asked me and because he seemed to have something in mind. Once we'd completed the circle, Mathew began to make a smaller one inside of the first, again by hauling over cobblestones of which some would've broken his foot had he dropped them. I followed along, walking here and there for likely looking stones and carting them back. Once we completed the second circle, Mathew began to form yet another one inside the other two. He still hadn't told me what we were doing, but I continued to help. By the end we had three concentric circles of rocks on the sand. Mathew got down on his knees and shifted several of them around to form an entryway into the very center.

Once he'd done that, he straightened up and scampered down the beach.

"Hey," I called after him, "where are you going now?"

He didn't answer but continued down the beach a ways to a pile of driftwood. He pulled out a small stick, then began looking around on the ground. For feathers, as it turned out. Probably from a seagull. He then pulled up a small strand of kelp and wrapped it around the feathers to attach them to the wood. I stood and watched as he brought the whole mess back, along with two smaller, fist-sized rocks that he had cradled in his shirt. He entered the circles and placed the rocks in the middle of the smallest one.

"What are you doing?" I asked

"It's a sacred story circle," he said.

"Tell me about it."

"What we'll do," he said, "is tell each other stories inside the sacred story circle. When you're telling a story, you have to pass the stick to the other person."

"All right," I said.

So we sat there together on the beach. It was the middle of the morning and no one was around, and we passed the stick with the feathers and the kelp back and forth and told each other stories. We just made them up. I hardly even remember what we said, but we must have sat there for at least an hour. When I think back on the whole scene, I am amazed: I sat in the sand with my nine-year-old son, and we told each other stories inside a sacred story circle. At the time I didn't make the connection between what Mathew and I were doing and the inscription on the Chumash memorial that links us to the past, to the land, and to our children. I was simply following along with his little game. But the special atmosphere of Hammond's Reef itself—the secluded beach, the mountains and the meadow, the small rocks and shells and feathers that visitors leave at the base of the monument as a tribute—all of it has worked on my imagination and memories over the years so that I have come to appreciate that one hour more than almost any other time I've spent at the beach, including innumerable surf sessions at the most famous breaks in the world. Mostly, I think, because it was an experience that I didn't expect to have, and one that has become inseparable from a special place and special person in my life. Since losing Mathew, those moments have resonated for me even more strongly.

Hammond's was our local break, no more than a five-minute drive down the hill. As we pulled into our driveway that day, I saw that Mathew had carried a rock back with him. It was one of the two smaller rocks that he'd placed in the center of the smallest circle. He placed it right outside our front door.

"Why did you bring that home?" I asked him.

"You know all those stories we told today, Dada? They're all inside that rock."

The sacred story circle. I've never been so stoked in my life. When we'd left that morning to visit Hammond's, I thought that I was doing a favor for my son by visiting the beach and maybe giving him a surf lesson. Little did I realize the gift that he had in store for me, one that I enjoy every time I think of Hammond's and tell this story in front of a group of people.

At some of these gatherings, oftentimes someone will ask, "What makes surfing so special?"

Although I usually know that question is coming, I never have a simple answer. The experience of surfing, like any strong sensation, is hard to organize into words. There's a certain amount of faith involved, I end up saying; that leap into the unknown that makes every new step in life worth taking. Part of the appeal of surfing is that you never really know what you're going to get. I walk down the beach—I have my board and my wax and certain hopes, but I never really know what's in store for me. I might ride five of the best waves of my life in half an hour. Or I might sit there for three hours and catch nothing. Normally we want to remove uncertainty from our lives, but surfing is all about uncertainty. That feeling of taking a risk, that leap of faith every time I jump into the ocean—these are what make surfing special.

Or I might tell them a story by way of an answer: There's a storm far out at sea sending invisible bands of energy my way. I stand on the beach and see that energy arrive in the form of ocean waves, much as *'aumakua*—guardian gods in Hawaiian culture—can appear in the form of sharks to interact with humans. But that is not their true form. When I catch one of those bands of energy, stand on top of the wave and look down, I see the world from a unique perspective. I feel connected to the world in a special way.

Everybody has something special they like to do. For me it's surfing. For you it could be anything that makes you feel useful or talented or loved. Whatever that activity is—drawing, taking care of someone in your family, solving a complex problem—you can take pride in it because not everyone can do what you can do. And if you set goals for yourself, there's no limit to where your talents can take you. Sometimes you only need to say it to yourself to realize that your dreams are possible. Sometimes simply writing them down—telling a story about them—can help make your dreams come true. Stories connect us to each other and to the broader universe. The sacred story circle my boy Mathew created will always connect me to him and to the beautiful meadow and Hammond's Reef. Tell your own story. Make your own story circle with someone you love.

I WILL . . .

Speaking with kids about their hopes and dreams, about what they want their lives to be, is one of the most rewarding things I do. I'll often give them an assignment afterwards, asking them to create their own Code. I tell them to take twenty minutes to write down all their goals, beginning every sentence with the words "I Will." I'm constantly blown away by the breadth of imagination, the level of sensitivity, and the abundance of hope that resonates in their answers.

This book is about promises, and the answers from these kids are promises they've made to themselves—about making a commitment to future action. We all have hope for a better future. Sometimes all you need to turn hope into action is to write your promises down and say them out loud—to make a promise to no one but yourself.

Following are some examples of answers I've gotten to this assignment over the years (with special thanks to Gordon Sichi of Anacapa School and Stuart Sweeney at the University of California at Santa Barbara). After reading these examples, you'll have an opportunity to write down your own goals, your own promises to yourself.

"I will express myself." —Ashleigh W.

"I will stop making assumptions." —Fatima L.

"I will always question the accepted way." —Nichole F.

"I will focus on the good things in my life and forget the bad."
    —Megan E.

"I will think about how my actions affect others around me
    and the planet." —Corrina R.

"I will never be too cool to do the things that I love." —David S.

"I will finish everything I start." —Dela H.

"I will never give up on myself." —Jessie P.

"I will dive into uncertain situations with confidence rather
    than fear." —Brennan L.

"I will do what I want with my life." —Elena A.

"I will fight through my failures and learn from them."
    —Niklas F.

"I will acknowledge my mistakes." —Alex C.

"I will not bound my dreams and aspirations to what is
    tangible." —Melissa F.

"I will never be ashamed of myself." —Brenda G.

"I will judge my success with my own standards."
    —Madeliene H.

"I will not hurt others to help myself." —Chelsea N.

"I will acknowledge that not everyone will like me." —Vanessa R.

"I will always be willing to learn." —Elijah W.

"I will improve when I lose." —Esai M.

"I will be different than everyone else." —Raymond J.

"I will not do what other people want me to do simply to
    please others." —Patrick A.

"I will prove to my mother that she can be proud of me by
    choice, not because we're related." —Morgan R.

"I will be better than my parents." — Vanessa R.

"I will not compare myself to others." —Nuraram G.

"I will respect others' opinions whether I think they are good or bad." —Auguste H.

"I will not be afraid." —Hazel B.

"I will not judge people I have not met or do not know." —Francis B.

"I will do what I say I will do." —Alex C.

"I will resolve my outstanding problems with the people I care about." —Sophie C.

"I will try something that I said I never would." —Odalys G.

"I will not do something simply for the satisfaction of others." —Genn H.

"I will never stop being 'artsy.'" —Nichole F.

"I will never be famous for rapping." —Haley Y.

"I will never turn down a friend in need." —Gazal H.

"I will try to the best of my abilities because trying is better than succeeding." —Emily J.

"I will always love what I do." —Charley K.

"I will attempt things I shouldn't." —Timmy J.

"I will always tell the truth even if I know the consequences." —Colin L.

"I will do one good deed every day without anyone knowing it was me." —Heather M.

"I will approach my seemingly impossible goals or tasks by chipping away at them a tiny bit at a time." —Ila R.

"I will give back to everyone who helped me." —Justin H.

"I will be more confrontational in situations where I need to be." —Megan E.

"I will live each day as if something important could happen." —Kateryna F.

Twelve promises:

1. _____

_____

2. _____

_____

3. _____

_____

4. _____

_____

5. _____

_____

6. _____

_____

7. _____

_____

8. _____

_____

9. _____

_____

10. _____

_____

11. _____

_____

12. _____

_____

ACKNOWLEDGMENTS

The authors wish to thank the students at Anacapa School in Santa Barbara, California, who welcomed Shaun and participated in his "I Will..." exercise; some of their responses inspired several of the lesson titles: Elena A., Patrick A., Emilia A., Grayson B., Auguste B., Hazel B., Julio B., Francis B., Alex C., Aiyana C., Sophie C., Chris E., Megan E., Hannah E., Nichole F., Odalys G., Zinnia G., Brenda G., Dela H., Genn H., Kassidy H., Gazal H., Emily J., Raymond J., Timmy J., Henry J., Lottie J., Charley K., Lara K., Colin L., Fatima L., Esai M., Isaac M., Heather M., Matthew N., Rufus O., Clayton P., Ali P., Ryan R., Jessica R., Rebecca R., Sandra R., Corrina R., Sam R., Ila R., Shayna S., Ethan S., Gracie S., Clayton P., Douglas T., Kiara T., Diego V., Elijah W., Ashleigh W., and Haley Y. We also wish to thank Anacapa's headmaster, Gordon Sichi, and his dedicated staff of teachers and advisors.

Special thanks to Marie Tomson, Carla Tomson, Tracy Tomson, Paul Tomson, Ernest Bongani Nkosi, and Linda Moser. We wish to thank our agent, Wendy Burton Brouws, and our editor, Bob Cooper, along with the rest of the creative team at

Gibbs Smith. A special thank you to Glenn Hening for his inspiration. Thanks also to the following media and photographers for contributing work: *New York Daily News, Natal Mercury,* Heidi Blair, Jeff Divine, Glenn Dubock, Dan Merkel, and Lance Trout.

The following works were helpful during the writing of this book: *The Teen Years Explained: A Guide to Healthy Adolescent Development* by Clea McNeely and Jayne Blanchard (Center for Adolescent Health at Johns Hopkins Bloomberg School of Public Health, 2009), *The Encyclopedia of Surfing* by Matt Warshaw (Houghton Mifflin Harcourt, 2003), *Bustin' Down the Door* by Wayne "Rabbit" Bartholomew and Tim Baker (HarperCollins, 1996), and the documentary *Bustin' Down the Door,* directed by Jeremy Gosch (2009).